Canal is King

A fascinating canal journey with a difference,

from idyllic tranquillity to urban city grunge.

By Bill Savage

Bill Savage

Email: wig.wam@gmx.com

CONTENTS

For the Navvy, Toerag and Gongoozler.

The Warwick Ring

Bill Savage

INTRODUCTION

The **Warwick Ring** is a circular canal route in the Midlands using five different canals, crossing four counties, connecting two cities, seven towns, and many hamlets and villages. It's around 115 miles long and I'm told travelling it by narrowboat takes between one and two weeks. I'm walking it, but not all in one go. I'll be doing it in bite-sized pieces, walking between idyllic rural tranquillity and industrial urban grunge. From Iron Age to Jet Age, William the Conqueror to the Peaky Blinders. We'll be discovering some interesting and unexpected finds, delving into canalsy goings on, talking with the characters we meet along the way and seeing where history happened. A few adventures and unfortunate mishaps inevitably occur, but nothing too serious.

ONE

WHY?

I discovered the Warwick Ring after having a bit of a brain wobble. For some reason which I am yet to fathom, I signed up to complete two half-marathons and three 10K races, climb Snowdon and the Yorkshire Three Peaks then, to top it all off, climb Mount Fuji - all to be completed in under a year. It was for charity and some very good causes, but I'm not very athletic and the only running I can remember doing was to get to the pub before it shut. As friends and family started to distance themselves from me as I asked for more and more charity donations, I realised this was something I could not back out of easily. So, I started to think about training and joined the local gym. Blimey, it was boring. Muscular blokes preening themselves in the mirror ignited my inferiority complex, whilst putting my body to shame and making me feel like a complete wimp. Running the local lanes wasn't much better. Cross country was more interesting, but the paths are not always easy to follow. I'd get lost and end up having challenging encounters with farmers or livestock or both. Then one day, to break the monotony, I decided to run to Warwick, my nearest town. It's around six miles away so perfect training for the 10K races. Instead of joining traffic along the busy main Birmingham Road, I looked for a less polluted route. Lo and behold, only a couple of miles away ... the canal. Why hadn't I thought of it before? It's quiet, it's pleasant, it's interesting, there's no traffic or preening blokes and I won't get lost or run over. Perfect.

After arriving in Warwick, I had a quick stroll around town, then turned and headed for home (no buses venture my way). Stopping at Hatton Locks Café for a cup of tea, I noticed a map for sale entitled "The Warwick Ring". I bought one and as soon as I saw the circular route, that was it. I set myself the task of running the whole circuit before the end of the year. I've used that map ever since, marking where I ended the last section and where to begin the next. I now complete the route at least once a year and for the first couple of years, I would drive and park the car at the allotted starting line, run a few miles, then turn around and run back. It was always important to select a turnaround point with vehicle access, so I had somewhere to park for the next section. In and out of Birmingham always involved public transport, but never anywhere else. Until now that is. To add to the challenge, I decided to run/walk the route clockwise, without turning back. It meant much longer journeys (15 miles or more) and lots of public transport, something I'm not familiar with or very good at.

I don't run the Ring anymore, walking it is enough for me now. Since I stopped running, the slower pace allows time for the occasional chat with people I meet along the way, whilst discovering much more about the canal and the local area. Why am I doing it? Well, as I've said before, I find any form of physical training mighty boring. But, taking on a challenge gets me off my backside and writing about it exposes another dimension. It's surprisingly fun and educational and makes physical exercise less boring and a bit more stimulating for the old grey matter.

Even though it's a circular route, there are a couple of interesting diversions and a choice of two routes to Birmingham. I'm not sure which one we will be taking just yet, and we may go off-piste occasionally if something piques our curiosity. So, what are we waiting for …? Let's go.

Two

Birmingham to Fazeley

15 miles

Bill Savage

Where to start this walk? I'm a Brummie, so it's obvious. Birmingham. First, though, we need to break the rules. I know I said "clockwise", but we're going to do this leg of the Warwick Ring (and only this leg) back to front - Fazeley to Birmingham - and it's a couple of trains and a bus ride to get to Fazeley to start the journey. Birmingham's Gas Street Basin to Fazeley Junction near Tamworth is around 15 miles along the Birmingham and Fazeley Canal. This section of the Warwick Ring is quite straight and uninspiring with not much going on until the outskirts of Birmingham. It's been drizzling all morning and now I see heavy rain clouds ahead. This should be fun.

A few minutes into the walk is Drayton Manor (now a theme park), built for Robert Peel, the man who gave his name to the British "Bobby". He was also elected Prime Minister twice, in 1834 and 1841. The canal runs through Drayton Manor Estate so the Drayton Footbridge, one of the most ornate on the U.K. canal network, was created for the wealthy industrialist, along with a swing bridge to allow livestock and farm traffic to cross.

DRAYTON FOOTBRIDGE WITH SWING BRIDGE BEHIND.

A lot has been said recently about "Red Tape", but what actually is it? The Robert Peel Mill (also known as Tolson's Mill) was built in 1883 for the sole purpose of manufacturing the red ribbon used to tie up legal documents. Imagine, a massive five storey, steam-powered factory just to make red tape. Unbelievable. It's derelict and now looking quite sad, and sure to be either bulldozed flat or refurbished. Either way, the whole site will end up as a residential waterside masterpiece any time soon. There were also dyeing and bleaching works, and three weaving mills in Fazeley, one of which is the best surviving Arkwright pattern mill, built in 1791. Richard Arkwright is known as the father of the modern industrial factory system.

We've just passed a chap wandering around looking slightly lost, but he seemed okay when I said "hello". Up ahead, I can just make out a couple on the towpath, also wandering around looking lost. Next, I nearly trip over a little pug dog wandering around and it looks lost too. Is there a connection? I put two and two together and quickly decide the man and the couple are looking for the same little pug dog at my feet and I'm going to help them repatriate. So, I make friends with pug dog and entice it to follow me towards the couple. After lots of silly dog talk and encouragement, we eventually reach the designer-clad, twenty-something couple who, by now are walking slowly, hand-in-hand and with an aura of luuuuuve surrounding them. I interrupt their "special moment" and say, "Excuse me, is this your dog?" In unison they stop, turn around, look at me, look down at the dog, then at me again, say "No", look at each other with a "what the hell?" expression, turn, face forward and walk on. I am left standing there, deflated, not knowing quite what to do. And with someone else's dog in my possession. Behind me, in the distance, I can see the "wandering around" man still looking lost and I now hear the faint call of a name. It sounds like "Pugsy", or is it "Thugsy"? No, it's "Mugsy". My new canine friend is called Mugsy. What to do now? I contemplate deserting the stupid little mutt. It can find its own way back. But it might follow me, and then what would I say to the loved-up couple when we overtake them? "Mugsy, my old pal, let's backtrack." Mugsy is not so enthusiastic now and struggling to breath. "That's one hell of a badly designed dogface you've got there little fella ... and whatever you do, DON'T POO ... I'm not picking it up." Eventually, after more doggy talk and the occasional kick up the bum, we reach Mugsy's very grateful owner and I make a hasty retreat. No more dog rescue duties for me. Next time, just walk on.

The canal meanders past Middleton Lakes and Kingsbury Water Park so I'm expecting to see plenty of interesting wildfowl. No luck today, not a dicky-bird, just a brace of engineers perched on an electricity pylon, with a couple more below. After passing underneath the M6 Toll road, the towpath becomes paved and wide. "Rural" slowly starts turning "urban"

PYLON REPAIRS NEXT TO BAYLIS'S BRIDGE

with 10 miles still to go before reaching Birmingham city centre. And it's just started to rain.

Walking past the Jaguar factory I'm reminded of the Spitfire, which was built in a shadow factory close by. (Shadow factories were developed in the mid-1930s as a means of using a skilled workforce to prepare for war.) Once complete, the aircraft would be moved across the road to Castle Bromwich Aerodrome for flight tests. The Lancaster Bomber was also built here and the site provided the main source of aircraft for the war effort. It's now Castle Vale housing estate, once a notorious sink estate and home to my grandma-in-law. Just a coincidence (I think). Castle Vale Estate was built in the mid-1960s with 34 high-rise blocks. As early as 1967 they showed signs of poor-quality build and substandard materials (corruption in high places is not exclusive to Banana Republics). By the 1980s, Birmingham City Council used it as a dumping ground for its most problematic and vulnerable citizens. It started to be demolished in the late 1990s and rebuilt. It's still a housing estate but only two of the original tower blocks remain.

Bridges along the Warwick Ring are usually numbered but the Birmingham and Fazeley Canal Company decided to name them. Double Bridge, Broad Bulk Bridge and Aston Railway Bridge are self-explanatory. Some are named after the factory they fed ... Cincinnati Bridge, Brace Factory Bridge and Gasworks Bridge. Or farms ... Cheatles Farm Bridge and Willdays Farm Bridge. Troutpool Bridge evokes a romantic image of 18th Century Brum. And then there is Saturday Bridge, which is thought to be where canal workers collected their wages every Saturday. Probably the ugliest bridge on the canal network is Erdington Hall Bridge with its monster factory sitting on top. It's more like a tunnel than a bridge. Budding graffiti artists practise their craft on the structural supports down here, mostly of men's genitalia. Banksy they're not. The old tunnels are amazing. Nothing stopped those 18th century engineers and navvies. Curdworth Tunnel, completed in 1794, is an early example of canal engineering and is now a listed "building". A couple of interesting features are the ridged brick "horse treads" to reduce slipping and the wrought iron safety rail to stop man or horse from accidentally falling in. It's around 52 metres long.

Fort Dunlop, built in the 1920s is another old industrial building located close to the canal and was once the biggest factory in the world. Dunlop made the first pneumatic tyre in Birmingham in 1901 and by the 1970s it was still the largest manufacturer of tyres outside of the USA. Sadly, in the 1980s, large-scale tyre production ceased with the factory closing in 2014 and production moving to Germany and France. For a long while, the building was a familiar sight when travelling the M6, being used as advertising space. It has now been converted for retail use, offices and a hotel.

A couple of months ago, a burglar fleeing the cops on a stolen motorbike crashed into the canal along here. He and another bloke were targeting pubs and smashing up vending machines for the money. Even with £300 worth of £1 coins in his pockets, he managed to drag himself out of the canal and was promptly arrested. An overhead police chopper caught it all on camera.

It's tipping it down as we pass where the Cincinnati factory once stood. I'm sure it was still standing last year but now there are smart looking, four-bedroom waterside properties and I'm

PASSING THE SITE OF THE CINCINNATI WORKS.

feeling sad as another Birmingham success story bites the dust. At its peak, Cincinnati employed over 2,000 people manufacturing machine tools, which graced workshops the world over. It closed in 2008, just one year after being sold. A union official said at the time "... they will not be getting away quietly with this". Production later moved to China.

At last, Spaghetti Junction. It's amazing underneath this monster. Canal on one side, River Tame on the other, and traffic thundering overhead. It's otherworldly and strangely peaceful. I love the modern urban grunge, which only gets better (or worse if you don't like graffiti) the closer to the city you get. Has it ever been used as a film set? Yes, it has. In 2016, Steven Spielberg used the location for his science fiction

SPAGHETTI JUNCTION ON ONE SIDE, CANAL ON THE OTHER.

film, "Ready Player One". The film is set in 2045, with the world on the brink of chaos and collapse. Spaghetti Junction was the perfect location.

Gravelly Hill Interchange (official title) first opened in 1972 and was the most complex, multilevel interchange in the world. Well done Brum. Another world first. Who needs a top-flight football club when we've got Spaghetti Junction. Talking of football clubs, you can see the Villa ground from the Expressway above us. Aston Villa Football Club was formed in 1874 and became the most successful club in the Victorian era. In their very first match, they played the first half by rugby rules and the second half by football rules. Oh, what a spectacle it must have been. If only that was the basis of today's game, I'd be a regular at Villa Park.

UNDER THE STREETS OF ASTON.

Once past Spaghetti Junction, the city starts to come into view, with the unmistakeable BT Tower on the skyline. The canal passes Saint Chad's Cathedral, the first catholic church to be built in the UK since the reformation, and on through an area that was once the most important firearms manufacturing centre in the world. The first recorded gunmaker here was in 1630, with their muskets being used in the English Civil War. By 1767 there were 35 gunmakers in Birmingham, but soon after WW2, production dried up as cheaper imports took over. The only evidence left of this historic trade is the Birmingham Gun Barrel Proof House, which continues its work and is occasionally open to visitors.

It's a quiet and peaceful world down here, hidden from the hustle and bustle above. The view changes from quaint, old world canal locks and bridges to serious concrete grunge ... and back again, with bridges turning into cavernous tunnels supporting vast city buildings above. Snow Hill Railway Bridge is enormous and as we pass a group of lads sitting on some steps, the sweet smell of weed hits my nostrils. It's a big area down here and they would blend into the gloom of the tunnel if it wasn't for the strong smell of wacky backy.

SNOW HILL RAILWAY BRIDGE

Not long ago, Police put out a warning to the public about this area. A group of young males were congregating around the tunnel late at night and in the early hours of the morning. They were threatening and robbing people. This kind of thing happens in any major city, the world over. Wherever you are, be alert, stay safe and avoid dodgy areas at night. Simple.

So here we are, under the mean streets of Birmingham, and I'm taking a picture of a pair of ancient lock gates with a graffitied up wall behind. It needs someone in the shot to make it more interesting, and there happens to be a young lady with rainbow coloured hair and a lovely big smile lurking in the shadows. When I ask her if she would help me out, she turns and shouts down the tunnel. Another young lady with a small amplifier, and a man carrying camera gear materialise from the shadows. Once they check me out to make sure I'm harmless, they tell me they're shooting a video of Kaycee Light (the smiling, rainbow girl) doing a bit of rapping. Kaycee tells me she's been rapping since she was nine. As they get into position for the photo, they suddenly change their persona and all strike a pose reminiscent of famous Gangsta Rappers … lots of attitude and snarling faces. Once I've finished taking the pictures, they turn back into normal people again, and I hang around for a while to experience Kaycee perform her Rap. I'm no judge of Rap music but it sounded brilliant to me. I say… "Like daht waz sikk Man, like init … like." Kaycee and the Crew put their snarling Rapper faces back on … they don't look very

KAYCEE LIGHT
(CENTRE) & HER CREW

impressed with my attempt at street talk. So, I offer my fist to be bumped and I say my farewells … "Like stay safe Bruv. Cheerio girls. Lovely to meet you … init". I just love gettin dahn wiv da kidz.

At the time of the Suez crisis in the 1950s, not far from here, work began on a stretch of secret underground bunkers to protect the chosen few from nuclear fallout. There are four tunnels, 150 feet deep, which stretch from the Jewellery Quarter (near the Birmingham and Fazeley Canal) to Deritend (near the Grand Union Canal).

From gun manufacturing, the canal takes us into the Jewellery Quarter. Today, it boasts the highest number of jewellery manufacturers in Europe, with over a third of all British jewellery being made within one mile of Birmingham City. The first reference to jewellery making in Birmingham was in 1553. Heavy metal bashing was concentrated north of the city, around the Black Country, whilst Birmingham handled metalwork where more precision and skill was required. Jewellery began to be made to improve profits and compliment the trade in small metal items, such as buttons, buckles, snuff boxes, toys and candlesticks. At least Birmingham still thrives in one of its many trades of the past. Testament to that is

Birmingham Assay Office, the largest in the world. Birmingham was also the centre of the World's pen and steel nib industry, and it was estimated that at one time, 75% of everything written in the world was written with a Birmingham pen. Unfortunately, a Hungarian named Lászió Biró invented the ballpoint pen just before the outbreak of WW2, and the pen business was never the same again. One Birmingham 19th Century business which does remain the largest in the world is whistle manufacturer J. Hudson & Co. Founded in the 1870's, their Acme whistle has been used by the Police, football referees and the crew of the Titanic, to name but a few.

With today's finishing line almost in sight, a very attractive lady, with a sexy foreign accent, asked me, "How do you get to the catacombs from here?" She sounded Spanish. Here's a chance to impress someone, anyone, with my immense knowledge of Birmingham. "Catacombs señorita? There's no catacombs around here Luv." In a flash, her male companion, who I'd not noticed before, sticks his phone in my face, and there they are. Birmingham's Catacombs. I quickly checked with Uncle Google and his map, and found out they are in the Jewellery Quarter, not far from the canal. I gave them directions, making a bad job of pretending I knew where they were all along. A few days later, I went looking for them and found them hidden within Warstone Lane Cemetery. I'm no fan of graveyards, and the place was extra spooky because it has not been used for years and the gravestones were at all angles, but it was remarkably peaceful. The cemetery opened in 1847 to cope with Birmingham's rapid increase in population (from around 11,000 in 1720 to 73,000 by the end of the century). The unhealthy stench emitted from these two storey catacombs caused the Council to bring in a new law, requiring non-interred coffins to be sealed with lead or pitch. If the area were tidied up a little, it would make a lovely, peaceful oasis for the Jewellery Quarter.

CATACOMBS IN WARSTONE LANE CEMETERY.

This section of the Warwick Ring always tweaks my consciousness. It cuts across so many familiar street level landmarks, but the view from the towpath has no cognitive connection. That doesn't stop hazy memories popping into my head as the finishing line approaches. Middleton ... mucking out horse stables for pocket money. Forge Lane ... some heavy petting and serious courting. Cuckoo Bridge ... failed driving test. Aston ... good customers and great characters. Gas Street and Brindleyplace ... amazing live music clubs like Opposite Lock, Fiddle & Bone and Barbarellas. I can't remember many of the details, but it was definitely far out man, groovy and fab. Oh, and later, the sadly missed Ronnie Scott's. Sensational.

BT TOWER & FARMERS BRIDGE FLIGHT OF LOCKS.

Farmers Bridge Locks are next. Once the busiest flight on the canal network, and lit with gas lights for night working, they would have been hemmed in by factories on all sides, and very congested. During recent restoration work, I managed to walk along the bottom of No.1 and No.2 locks to see how these things were built. Wow, they were in amazing condition and not quite what I expected for a couple of 230 year old's.

FARMER'S BRIDGE LOCK No.1

We've now reached Brindleyplace and Gas Street Basin, the end of this leg of the walk. Brindleyplace, once a canal side road, was named after canal engineer James Brindley who was the architect of much of Birmingham's early canal system. During the canal era, Gas Street would have been a very busy area and so became the first place in the city to get gas lighting. The basin was the junction for the Birmingham Canal and the Worcester & Birmingham Canal and competition between the two companies meant a physical barrier was created (called the Worcester Bar). The whole area would have been teeming with activity, surrounded by wharves, warehouses and factories. Birmingham canals survived through the railway age but as road transport improved after the Second World War, the basin became unused and unloved. In the 1990s the area was in a sorry state, with a mixture of derelict industrial buildings and stagnant canals filled with old tyres and bicycles and other such debris. I remember it well. Disgusting. Luckily, Birmingham had the right people in place at the right time and instead of concreting over the cesspit, civic bosses with vision transformed the area into a hub for shopping, leisure and nightlife. This canal and towpath area is pretty cool now, with pubs, bars, coffee shops and restaurants aplenty. I often stop here awhile, people and narrowboat watching; there's so much going on. The area now attracts 10,000 visitors a day and boasts Symphony Hall, International Convention Centre, Indoor Arena, Sea Life Centre and Legoland to name just a few attractions. Beggars have become commonplace in this area now, due to the large number of visitors and pedestrian through traffic. It's much the same in most UK cities these days.

Some of Birmingham's old canal buildings are being preserved and reinvented. Let's take a look at the Roundhouse, near Sheepcote Street Bridge. Originally called Corporation Wharf, it was built in 1873-74 and is an intriguing, crescent shaped building, originally used as a canal-side stables and stores. At the time of writing, it is in the process of being redeveloped. The Canal & River Trust say it will become; "A hub to explore the city by bike, boat or on foot". I can't wait.

ROUNDHOUSE.

It's still just good old Brum to me though, so, before catching the train home, I'm off for a wander around to see what all the fuss is about.

APPROACHING BRINDLEYPLACE FROM GAS ST BASIN

GAS STREET BASIN WHERE BEGGARS ARE COMMONPLACE.

THREE

FAZELEY TO NUNEATON

16 MILES

Bill Savage

Continuing the Warwick Ring Canal Walk, we're heading for Nuneaton along the Coventry Canal. Fazeley Junction is where the Birmingham and Fazeley Canal, and the Coventry Canal meet, and it's where we begin this leg of the trip. An early start and rush hour public transport got me here, but I've yet to work out how I'm getting home. Nuneaton is around 15 miles away so plenty of time to work something out.

A train got me to Birmingham's New Street Station (which is now more retail Mecca than railway station) then a bus to Fazeley. As I get off the bus, a poster stuck on the door of a derelict shop catches my eye. It's asking a provocative question ... "Who will protect us when the Police break the law?" Fair question. They're a radical bunch around here.

Not long after leaving Fazeley, the canal flows through an aqueduct (built around 1785), above the River Tame. This river feeds Europe's largest sewage treatment works at Minworth and flows underneath Spaghetti Junction. On the other side of the towpath I can see a WW2 pillbox. Around 18,000 of these defence structures were built within nine months after the evacuation of Dunkirk. In total, 28,000 were built across the UK, and around 6,500 now survive. There are a few keen fishermen along the towpath and one fella, whose as cocky as a sparrow, tells me his wife thinks he's at work and he does this regularly. Living dangerously I'd say. We're doing the walk on a day when the sky turned a weird orange pink colour and looked like something out of a sci-fi movie. Storm Ophelia is making her presence felt too, and the whole experience is a little surreal.

There are some great, spooky looking boat wrecks along here. At a small boatyard there is an interesting find, the only remaining horse-drawn tank boat. The Gifford was built in 1926 using oak and elm timber. She is 72 feet long and 7 feet wide and was originally used to transport tar around the Midlands. Later, she carried fuel oil from the Manchester Ship Canal to the Midlands Black Country and from around 1940 was towed by motorboat instead of horse. She ceased working in 1963. I'm not sure what she's doing here, but let's hope someone is taking care of her for posterity. Now here's a funny looking little boat sitting out of water in a boatyard. It has a name plate on it … "BANTAM 48". It's a tug. These craft were built from the late 1940's until the 1960's and were designed for pushing, not towing. They were used in gravel pits and canals. A couple of magnificent looking narrowboats are moored at the next boat yard along the way. These are another rare find, because they are carrying commercial goods and it looks like bags of gravel and sand. One boat is named "Australia". That's an odd name for a Coventry Canal barge. What's the story?

GIFFORD TANK BOAT

BANTAM 48 TUG

AUSTRALIA AND ANOTHER BOAT

How do people choose boat names anyway? I've seen "India" and Portugal" around here, and quite a few have been cobbled together using partners' names. Bob and Sue = "Subo". There are plenty of boats named after birds. "Heron" and "Kingfisher" are popular. You can work out the age of boat owners when song titles are used. "My Way" and "Mr. Blue Sky" are regulars around here. There's also "Flat Bottomed Girl" and "Argi Bargi". How's this for originality; "Aquaholic". My favourite is "On Reflection". The name is painted as a mirror image on the hull and appears to reflect in the water not up-side-down, but the right way up. That's clever.

What an amazing autumn day for the walk. The sky is still a crazy pinkie-orange and storm Ophelia is bearing down, shaking trees and chasing leaves across the rippled water. The sound is deafening and it's starting to feel a little isolated and mysterious. At least I can hear the trains are still running. The canal criss-crosses the busy London to Manchester railway line, and it will be a constant companion all the way to Nuneaton then on to Rugby, which is our next destination after we've finished this leg.

We've reached Polesworth, which last year was voted (by me) the place with the most miserable people on the towpath and won my "Misery Guts On The Cut" award. I always say "hello" to all who pass and usually get a cheery wave, or at least a half-hearted grunt. But here, only an angry face looking like a dog's bottom. So far today though, everyone is saying "hello" and waving back. Coal mining, quarrying and brickworks feature in the recent history of Polesworth, together with a thriving pottery industry and a large boatyard to service the busy canal traffic. In the 11th century, a Benedictine Abbey was established which, to avoid bloodshed, was surrendered to King Henry VIII in 1539 after his fallout with the Pope. Religion has always been a bloodthirsty business.

There have been a few suicides and murders along the Warwick Ring. There was one in 1886, when a young man dived in to save Miss Emma Salmon, who was desperately trying to kill herself. She fought with him, grabbing hold of his throat, and managed to get away. When he eventually clambered out of the cold canal, he found Miss Salmon's body floating in the water. Another was in 1883, when 17-year-old Sarah Davies was found dead in the canal. At first her boyfriend, William Ellis was accused of her murder. His story was that as they walked arm-in-arm along the towpath, she suddenly held onto him tightly and dived into the water, taking him with her. He couldn't swim but managed to get out. She drowned. The jury found William Ellis not guilty. And then there is the sad but funny (I think so anyway) case of Henry Cundy who, in 1900, attempted suicide by jumping off Salford Bridge, missing the canal and landing on the pavement. This was his third attempt. A more recent incident was in 2004, when PC Michael Swindells gave chase to a man carrying a knife. Tragically, he was stabbed to death when he caught up with the suspect along the canal towpath. There is a memorial stone to the memory of D.C. Swindells at the spot where he was attacked and died. Walking past it, I always wonder how a known, dangerous and paranoid schizophrenic could be out roaming the streets, and not in a secure psychiatric hospital, getting proper help and keeping the general public, and Michael Swindells safe from harm. No doubt, whoever was responsible at the time said "lessons will be learnt" or something similar. I'm sure these platitudes are no comfort to family and friends.

Along this section of the canal a couple of years back, I decided to stop for an early lunch. Benches are scarce along the towpath, so when I spotted one just past a few moored-up boats, I made myself comfortable and started to unpack sandwiches from my rucksack. As I happily munched away, enjoying the beautiful summer morning and peaceful setting, a bloke materialised from one of the boats. He was wearing shorts and sandals but nothing else. Then another bloke in shorts and sandals but nothing else also appeared on deck. Judging by the muscles popping out of the tanned, tattooed, perfect body of the second bloke, he must have spent most of his adult life at the gym. He was about mid-thirties and his chubby, pale skinned pal, probably mid-forties. To my astonishment, two more blokes emerged from one of the other boats, also in shorts and sandals. All four blokes eventually gathered together on the towpath for a smoke and a chat, whilst I nonchalantly chomped on my sandwiches. As I pulled a banana from my rucksack and started to peel it, one of the blokes walked past me and glared. He stopped at the last boat, the one nearest to me, and banged on the roof. As he passed me to return to his friends, he glared again. This time, I had the banana in my mouth and for some reason, found the situation hilarious and struggled not to explode with laughter. What is it about eating bananas in public, especially in front of half naked men. I then remembered something comedian Peter Kay once said ... "You never know where to look when eating a banana." Anyway, our eyes met as he passed and I tried a friendly smile, whilst stifling a giggle and munching away at the banana. I must have looked slightly insane. He averted his eyes, quickened his step and when he reached his friends, after a few brief words, they all turned to stare at me in a very unfriendly way. Hearing a noise coming from the nearest boat, I saw another half naked bloke emerge into the morning sunshine, followed by one of the ugliest human specimens I've ever laid eyes on, unfortunately also half naked. This pair were probably in their early fifties. They both looked like heavy drinkers and, judging by the smell of a brewery escaping from their boat into the clean morning air, alcohol was probably the culprit for destroying their youthful good looks. I said "good morning" in the cheeriest manner I could muster, and they slowly turned and focused on me, grunted, looked at one another with a vacant gaze, then carefully shuffled back to their beery cabin in silence whilst randomly scratching various body parts. It was time for me to leave, so I packed up my things and started walking. After a few steps, I turned for a last look at the weird world I had just left, and three of the blokes were now sitting on the bench, with the ugly one delicately clambering out of his boat with a six pack (beer not body) in hand. Then I realised why the unfriendly vibes. I was sitting on their bench. As I walked on, I couldn't help but wonder what the bloody hell was going on. Was it a gay thing? Was it an alcoholics meetup? Was it a bodybuilders convention? Or just a bunch of mates having fun? At least the encounter taught me one thing, and ever since, I've taken Peter Kay's advice. Bananas must be consumed with care.

It's not only the railway following the canal, the River Anker and Watling Street (the old Roman Road, now the A5) pop up from time to time. Canal, river, rail and Roman road all go through Atherstone, which has a long, rich history going back to Roman times. Atherstone is recorded in the Doomesday Book of 1086, with Countess Godiva (Coventry's naked Lady Godiva no less) as the Head Honcho. It's thought the Battle of Bosworth (English Civil War) was not fought in Bosworth at all but here in Atherstone. The slave trade was good business for Atherstone. The town was a major hat producer since Tudor times, employing over 3,000 people and the billycock hat was exported in vast quantities to slave owners in British colonies the world over. Abolition of the slave trade in 1807 caused great hardship for the town and the hat trade eventually ceased with the last hat-maker closing in 1999. Atherstone also produced leatherwork, various cloths, metalwork, tanning,

ATHERSTONE OLD
FACTORY BUILDINGS.

shoes and a hell of a lot of ale. Some of the old factories and warehouses still remain along the canal but look dilapidated. No doubt they'll soon be demolished and replaced with swanky waterside homes.

Have you ever heard of the Pamplona Bull Run in northern Spain? It's where bulls rampage through the narrow streets every year, trying their best to gore people to death. Well, Atherstone has a similar event staged every Shrove Tuesday, using ball instead of bull. In 1199, teams from Warwickshire and Leicestershire fought for a bag of gold and the game has been played here every year ever since. The game was common in many English towns. It lasts for two hours and the only rule appears to be that no one should die. The bag of gold was eventually substituted for a large leather ball that would often end up in the canal, so now the main street in town, Long Street, is where the brawl takes place. Schools, shops and businesses close early, windows are boarded up and brave chaps in hi-vis jackets attempt to keep order. I once visited the town to see for myself. Yes … it's utter mayhem and almost primal. The winner is whoever has the ball at the end of the game. Whilst paramedics and coppers stand by, tanked up thugs knock seven bells of crap out of one another. Although it seems absolutely pointless, it's obviously a great excuse for a right royal punch up, sandwiched between more than a few bevvies. Covered in blood and gore, participants, along with their tribe, return to their chosen tavern and continue drinking copious amounts of ale until the next Shrove Tuesday comes about. Sadly, there wasn't a pancake in sight.

ATHERSTONE BALL GAME.

Gazing across the canal a little further along the towpath, I am imagining the scene of a spectacular battle where around 80,000 British and 4,000 Romans fought to their deaths. This was AD59 and Queen Boudica's last battle to keep Britain free and where she probably died. The landscape fits in well with what is known about the battle, especially with the Roman Road being close by.

It seems I'm not the only freak travelling the canals. The other day I bumped into a guy who was walking from London to Birmingham. He would walk for a day, catch the train back home and start again from where he last finished. I met him just outside Solihull, about 12 miles from Birmingham City Centre and the end of his trip. That's similar to our walk, only linear. On another occasion, I met a couple cycling from Manchester to London. They were looking for a B&B for the night. The lady was grumbling about her sore backside and didn't look at all happy, whilst her partner was more interested in showing me his new panniers and completely ignored her complaints. I wonder if they're still together? The last time I walked this section I came across a chap sitting on the bank with his head in his hands and looking pretty down and out. I asked him if he was okay and he told me he'd started out first thing and was headed for Rugby, another 17 miles of walking. He'd got a job interview but had no money for the train fare. He had water but no food so I rummaged around in my bag and found a packet of beef jerky, a Snickers bar, some peanuts and a banana. Quite a feast. He gratefully accepted the gift once I lied about having plenty of supplies in my rucksack. He could have been telling me a pack of lies. Who knows? Anyway, he seemed to perk up a bit so I said "cheerio" and wished him good luck for the interview. I hope he got the job.

Just past the Anchor Inn in Hartshill is Jee's Hill named after the local family who owned it. Standing around 130 metres high, it comprises spoil from a quarry. This landscape changed forever in the 16th century when granite and quartzite was discovered and with the advent of the motor vehicle, business boomed, keeping pace with road improvement. The area attracts a variety of interesting wildlife now that it's just picturesque hills and lakes, all man-made of course.

Nuneaton is not far now, which reminds me... who's never heard of Nuneaton's most famous daughter, Mary Anne Evans? Better known by her pen name, George Eliot. Film Director Ken Loach and Mary Whitehouse, who campaigned against sex and violence on TV, were also born in Nuneaton, our next and last destination for today. Time to start thinking about how to get home.

Nuneaton at last, and this leg of the Warwick Ring Canal Walk is complete. Most memorable bits? My encounter with six half naked men and a banana. Realising that ordinary people in an ordinary town in the middle of ordinary England could be so dependent on the disgusting business of slave trading. And of course Storm Ophelia and the crazy sky. Anyway, Uncle Google and his trusty map tell me the way home and there's just enough time for a swift half before the next bus leaves. Result.

FOUR

NUNEATON TO RUGBY

18 MILES

Bill Savage

It's a very early start today. The intention is to see the sun rising as a backdrop to the towpath and canal. The bus to Nuneaton is a fifteen-minute drive away and I can see ground frost and low-lying mist through the headlights. Perfect for some interesting photos, but too early and too dark to see any colour in the sky just yet.

I'm getting the hang of this public transport malarkey. The bus stop timetable tells me my bus should be here in seven minutes. Here it comes and I'm on. I nonchalantly flash my "Licence To Travel FREE Bus Pass" at the driver who carefully inspects it. "I've never seen one this early." says he. Wow ... a valuable antique. Feeling pretty chuffed, I go to sit down. "You're too early mate ... not valid 'til nine thirty." No problem ... Contactless? "Nope." Apple Pay? "Nope." Cash? "Yup." .... so I give him a tenner. "Gotta be exact change mate." Oh! As I contemplate my predicament, a nice lady on the bus offers to change it. I pay the driver. As we pull away, I bump into some unexpected bus paraphernalia and at the very same moment, a car on the street lights up like a Christmas tree. It takes a few precious seconds for my eyes to tell my brain it's MY car ... and a few more precious seconds for my brain to tell my hand to grab the key fob from my trouser pocket and lock the car before it's too far away. Phew, that was close. The driver is clearly enjoying this early morning entertainment.

THE KIND LADY.

Apart from the kind lady, the bus is empty, so I get comfortable and we start chatting. She gives me her medical history, going into details I didn't really want to know. Changing the subject, I tell her I'm off to Nuneaton. "This bus doesn't go to Nuneaton" she tells me. STOP THE BUS! And with uncontrollable laughter, the driver lets me off at the next stop. Idiot! (Me, not him). I carefully check the timetable at my new bus stop and yes, number 55 goes to Nuneaton. There's one due in twelve minutes. It's on time and luckily, I've now got plenty of change (thank you, Kind Lady). I check my watch and the sky and imagine all those stunning sunrise photos I'll soon be taking. As it gets lighter and later it slowly dawns on me … this bus is making a broad sweep of all villages, housing estates and shopping centres within a three-mile corridor to Nuneaton. Oh no ... I'm on the slow bus ... what a flippin' disaster. It can't possibly get any worse. Can it? Oh well, another lesson in public transport protocol. Here's some advice for free ... avoid number 55 buses if you're in a hurry.

At last, the canal. Yippeee. It's ten to seven and we're starting where the last leg of the walk finished, Bridge 21. Rugby is approximately 17 miles away and, except for Bedworth, there's not much in the way of town or village in between. It's pretty rural but we'll have the M6 motorway for company for a while, as it runs parallel. Continuing, we go under the M6, M69 and M6 again, until we meet the Fosse Way, an old Roman Road linking Exeter with Lincoln. Coventry is omnipresent.

The canal is so calm this morning and there are a few early risers on the towpath. Duck feeder, dog walker, cyclist and fisherman. As we pass and exchange goodmornings, the duck feeder and dog walker say the same thing in a very cheery kind of way ... "Good morning ... best part of the day ..." I'd usually agree, but not today, not after my bus disasters.

Nuneaton is known locally as "Treacle Town". Local lad and camp comedian Larry Grayson joked about Apricot Lil from the jam factory. I'm old enough to remember his other friend, Slack Alice - from the pit? Anyway, no one knows the exact location but, a Victorian jam and treacle factory operated from somewhere in town.

Coal mining was massive around here; it was home to some of Britain's largest pits and plenty of coal still remains. Not far is Daw Mill Colliery, which closed in 2013 after an underground fire. Coal mining started here in the 13th century and peaked in 1939 when 5.8 million tons of coal was extracted. That's one hell of a carbon footprint. Without canals, the Industrial Revolution would never have happened. Canals were vital, transporting the vast amounts of coal coming out of the ground, fuelling the Industrial Revolution and feeding the monster that eventually ate them ... the Steam Engine.

We soon reach Marston Junction and pass the Ashby Canal, joining us from the north and connecting the coalfields of Ashby de la Zouch with this 18th century superhighway. Now we skirt past Bedworth, where recently a hoard of Iron Age gold coins was found, the third find in less than twenty years. Once a big coal mining centre, attracting migrants from all over the UK, Ireland and, more recently, the Indian subcontinent, Bedworth was also a major producer of gauze ribbon, bricks and lime.

MARSTON
JUNCTION

It's fascinating what you see at the bottom of people's gardens backing onto the canal. Did you know The Stig, Ghostface and Field Marshal Montgomery all live in Bedworth? To entertain passers-by, three gardens in a row have dummies of these famous characters. They're probably trying to outdo each other. If you've got a canal at the bottom of your garden, why not?

Just north of Coventry is Hawkesbury Junction, also known as Sutton Stop, a traditional mooring for working narrowboats. This is where the Coventry Canal and the Oxford Canal meet and run parallel for a while. We need to join the Oxford Canal but it's not obvious there are actually two canals here. I've been caught out before and ended up in Coventry so I'm ready for any canal shenanigans this morning. The reason they run parallel is due to a short-lived dispute back in 1779 between the Coventry Canal Company and the Oxford Canal Company over toll fees. These two canals exist because Coventry businessmen wanted a link to the nearby coalfields, London and the north, so pioneering canal engineer James Brindley was brought in for the job. The first major cargo to arrive at Coventry Canal Basin in 1769 was coal, and vast amounts of it helped Coventry to compete head on with their giant neighbour, Birmingham.

I missed my caffeine hit this morning and I'm gagging for a coffee, but the Greyhound Inn on the other side of the canal is shut. Back in the day, this area would be teeming with activity. Imagine the sounds and smells. Stable straw, horse wee and dung, smoky fires, pipe and cigarette tobacco, water lapping, blokes shouting, dogs barking, cats screeching, horses neighing, clanging and banging, cussing and swearing, coughing and spitting, belching and farting. Glorious. And the pub would be doing a roaring trade. This area is full of canal history and definitely worth a visit. Pub lunch at the Greyhound methinks. It's not even nine yet, so I'll save it for another day.

HAWKESBURY
JUNCTION

What's that man doing pushing a wheelbarrow with a big fridge in it along the tow path? Strange goings on so early in the morning. Not that long ago, access to the towpath was difficult for the general public. It was not a public right of way and was an offence to ride horse or bike without a permit. Around the next bend we come to a large, frost covered grassy bank next to the canal where, unexpectedly, a pony is staked out on a long rope and is happily grazing. "Good morning Little Pony. What are you doing here all alone? It's a bit frosty this morning ... are you warm enough? Will you be towing a narrowboat later? Here, let me give your ears a scratch ... and your neck a pat ... and your muzzle a rub. Oh, you like that. Sorry, I've got nothing for you to eat, and as much as I'd like to stay chatting, Rugby awaits. It was a pleasure meeting you Little Pony. Have a nice day ... Bye-bye."

The Oxford Canal is one of the oldest in Britain and was built to create a route to transport coal to Oxford, and on to London via the River Thames. It was opened in sections between 1774 and 1790 and was hugely successful until the arrival of the Grand Junction Canal, later to be part of the Grand Union Canal. It was designed by canal engineer James Brindley to form part of his grand plan to connect the rivers Thames, Trent, Mersey and Severn. Brindley used the contours of the land to navigate the route of the canal, resulting in a very bendy path and lengthy journey. Between 1829 and 1834 some of these bends were straightened out, shortening the route by thirteen and a half miles, and helping the canal to compete with the railway. The bendy sections are clearly visible today, with some interesting "off-road" loops, boatyards and tranquil moorings.

TRANQUIL MOORING.
PART OF THE OLD
CANAL

I'm a little surprised to see a bunch of old cars dumped on the other side of the canal. Morris Minor, Beetle, Volvo, VW Transporter, Mini, Porsche, Ferrari. PORSCHE? FERRARI? What are they doing here? I've had a few Minis in the past. Oh, that awful gear stick. You stirred it around until you found a willing and consenting gear that liked you enough to engage. If it happened to be reverse, you were rewarded with a truly terrifying noise as cogs screamed in protest. Anyone who has ever driven an old style Mini will know exactly what I mean. I've never got anywhere near a Ferrari though.

There is a noisy motorway close by. It must be the M6 and what's this? A trail off the towpath heading towards the noise. A quick detour and we're on a footbridge crossing the M6 motorway with busy traffic speeding underneath. The path appears to go nowhere in particular. Oh well. Back to the canal. Another regular noise is the hoot and whooooooosh of fast trains close by. London to Manchester Virgin trains are a regular companion, popping up from time to time all along this route. I stop for a snack under the M6 bridge, where canal, road and rail track converge, waiting for a narrowboat and train to come through at the same time. It would make a good picture, three forms of transport spanning 250 years. Nothing today. Maybe next time.

VIRGIN TRAIN TO LONDON.

Uh-oh ... swans on the towpath. They can be a real menace, especially when they've got young'uns. Have you ever heard of anyone getting their arm broken by "one blow from a swan's wing"? Bringing the subject of swans into any conversation will guarantee this well-known fact being quoted. But is it a myth? The last time I came across swans on the towpath it was very narrow and there was no way around. They made it clear they didn't want to let me pass, so I backtracked until I found a way through the hedge and tramped over a couple of tricky fields, escaping a gang of frisky bullocks until finding a way back to the towpath. Last year, a pair of swans built a nest right next to the towpath, laid six or seven eggs in it and a chap from the local factory visited every lunchtime to feed them. I'm taking no chances today and giving mum, dad and their teenage twins a wide berth.

Not far from the canal is Coombe Abbey, dating back to the 12th Century. It's now a hotel and country park. Back in the day, 1539 to be exact, King Henry VIII "appropriated" it for himself. Then, in 1603, Princess Elizabeth, daughter of James 1st, came to live here. But in 1605, Guy Fawkes (yes, he of the Gunpowder Plot) thought it might be a bit of a laugh if he kidnapped the Princess and put her on the throne after assassinating her father. Alas, the plot was foiled. Lancelot 'Capability' Brown redesigned the gardens and land in 1771 and his work can still be admired today.

Newbold Tunnel was built in 1829 as part of the canal-straightening project, a bit like today's road widening schemes I suppose. This 230-metre-long tunnel is very rare, because of its two towpaths and large size. I went looking for the old tunnel and eventually found it behind a couple of gravestones in St. Botolph's Church graveyard. Spooky. It's a fair distance from the new canal and I did have to explain myself to an important-looking, dog walking busybody patrolling the church grounds, who wanted to know what an oik like me was doing prowling his graveyard. He reminded me of Simon Cowell, with the same kind of punchable face. I felt like telling him to mind his own business, but instead, got him and his dog involved in the search for the mysterious tunnel. When we eventually found it, he got quite excited. So much for local knowledge. The River Avon and Newbold Quarry are close by. The quarry became a reservoir for canal water and is now a nature reserve.

NEWBOLD OLD TUNNEL

At last, signs of human life and canalsy goings-on as we get closer to Rugby. The thing about walking a towpath is, there's no need for map or compass, no matter how desolate or deserted the landscape. Following a canal will always lead to civilisation. As mentioned before, some sections of the old bendy Oxford Canal were left intact after the straightening project and a few offshoots can be seen here, creating a need for more bridges. Either side of Newbold Tunnel are a couple of identical cast iron beauties, designed with channels along the top rail to allow ropes to pass through as the horse goes over the bridge and the narrowboat continues its journey in the water below. This design of bridge, manufactured by Horseley Ironworks in Tipton, in the Black Country, became very popular and can be found on many canals in the U.K. They also built railway bridges, locomotives, all manner of steam engine and the first ever iron steamship (the *Aaron Manby*). The ship was made in sections so that it could be transported from the Midlands to London for assembly. It then sailed across the Channel to Le Havre and up the River Seine to Paris. Horseley Ironworks was an exceptional company, employing many people and exporting all over the world. They closed in 1991 and the site was redeveloped and turned into a housing estate.

Judging by the artwork depicting rugby players under the next bridge, Rugby Town is not far. The game of rugby was invented here when William Webb Ellis broke all the rules of football by picking up and running with the ball. The rest is history. The big lesson here, which no one appears to promote is, breaking rules can be a good thing. Rugby is now played the world over in one form or another and it all started here. And don't they know it. It's rammed down your throat at every turn. Street art, road names, buildings, parks, pubs, cafés. Webb Ellis this, Webb Ellis that. Probably a different story if they'd chosen another name for it. For goodness sake people, it's only a silly game, get over it. (I wouldn't dare say that in earshot of any rugby players - I'm not that stupid.)

Rugby School, where the game of rugby was invented (yes, we know ... thank you) has a list of ex-pupils showing what they got up to after leaving school. Wow! Very, very, very impressive. There are hundreds, many with "Sir" in front of their name, and all high-fliers. Interestingly, the "Sirs" are predominantly from the world of politics including Neville Chamberlain. Here's just a few listed under "Literature"; Salman Rushdie, Rupert Brooke (First World War poet), Lewis Carroll (real name Charles Lutwidge Dodgson), of *Alice in Wonderland* fame and Thomas Hughes, who wrote *Tom Brown's School Days*. What was it Nelson Mandela said? ...

"Education is the most powerful weapon which you can use to change the world." Just out of interest, I checked for famous people from my old school. Maybe they've not got around to publishing the list yet.

Coming into Rugby, just past the Old Leicester Road viaduct is Brownsover Hall, now a Hotel and once used by Frank Whittle (inventor of the turbo jet engine), and his design team during their jet engine testing days. This Victorian Gothic mansion is said to be haunted by a former resident, known as "one-handed Boughton". He apparently lost his arm during Elizabethan times. In the 18th century, clergymen successfully removed the spirit by getting it to climb into a bottle (really?), which was then chucked into a lake in the grounds. When fishermen recovered a container from the lake in the 1880s, haunting returned and now staff and guests have reported all sorts of spooky goings-on. Talking about ghosts, I met my first ever ghost hunter a few months back. I was exploring a stretch of canal I'd never walked before and got chatting to a chap who was quite knowledgeable about the area. After getting a bit of info, I asked him what he was doing along this stretch of canal. "Hunting ghosts" he told me, as if it was the most normal thing in the world to be doing. His name is Mel and he is a Ghost Hunter, checking out empty buildings for any signs of ghosts. He said he would be investigating a disused railway track for excessive spookiness later. Blimey ... that's one hell of a weird hobby.

This leg of the Warwick Ring Canal Walk is almost over and I'm thinking ... "Have I learned anything today?" Sure. Bus travel is not as easy as it looks, dawn is a wondrous time of day, ponies don't talk and if all children got a little closer to the standard of education at Rugby School, the possibilities could be stratospheric.

I've checked with Uncle Google and his map and it's time to leave the towpath and head for Rugby Train Station, about a twenty-minute walk away. I could catch the bus but there's no way after today's humiliation. So, it's the fast train to Coventry to pick up the car. Oh, no, the car! Was I quick enough with the key? Will it still be there? How many wheels will it have? Is a tramp living in it now? I'm really starting to fret.

FIVE

RUGBY TO STOCKTON

17 MILES

Bill Savage

L eamington Spa, the next town from Rugby, is about 26 miles away, but it's winter now and the journey is too far to complete in daylight (that's my excuse, anyway). The canal runs close to the village of Stockton, around 17 miles away and luckily, it's on a bus route with the first bus leaving at 07.40 a.m. Perfect.

Car key safely packed away, correct change ready, and the sign on the bus says "RUGBY". No bus dramas today, but it's standing room only and rammed full of surprisingly well-behaved schoolkids. We're soon in Rugby, so let's grab a coffee before setting out to find Bridge 59, where we ended the last trip. Rugby is just starting to wake up, which is more than can be said for the shop doorway rough sleepers. It's about a 30-minute walk to the canal, along a pedestrian route and over a very long footbridge that crosses a surprising number of railway lines. Rugby is bigger than I thought. To pass the time, I'm imagining where William Webb Ellis got his idea of picking up and running with the ball. I'm guessing he visited Atherstone one Shrove Tuesday to buy a Billycock hat and got mixed up in their Ball Game riot. At the first opportunity, he tried it out with his school chums, and the rest is history.

Frank Whittle invented the turbojet engine in Rugby. Quite an achievement and something the townsfolk should be proud of. I'm on the lookout for streets or pubs or statues or anything bearing his name. Frank was a very noisy neighbour, with residents complaining about the racket, forcing him to move to a more remote location in town. Maybe that's why no one wants to be reminded of him. The really noisy stuff happened down the road in the village of Lutterworth.

This is it, Bridge 59 ... and we're off. The weather forecast said "overcast" so why am I walking into blinding winter sunshine? I can't see a thing. Is that a bridge ahead? As I walk into the shade of the bridge, artwork comes into focus underneath. More rugger propaganda and Frank doesn't get a look in.

Even with two major railway lines and the M45 motorway cutting across the canal, this is the most rural section of the Warwick Ring. Not much history, no city renewal or urban grunge, one village, one hamlet and the occasional farm all the way to Stockton. Simply miles of flat, open farmland all around, probably unchanged for hundreds of years, and one of the most sparsely populated areas of Warwickshire. On days like today, especially when it's cold and I'm walking alone, it can get pretty boring. Often, my mind starts to wonder, and random songs from the past pop into my head and won't leave until I've belted them out at full volume. There's no risk of annoying anyone (except the cows and sheep) with my terrible voice, and it's amazingly cathartic. This is embarrassing though, but I'm going to tell you anyway. A catchy little song, which regularly interrupted the boring bits of a walk, has a chorus which went something like this;

"Take your time, my lovely old lad, there ain't no need to hurry, as long as you're able to wind up my clock, I have no need to worry."

I had no idea what it meant or where it came from, but it was forever invading my brain and driving me crazy. So, one day after arriving home from a long walk, with my brain frazzled by this song, I googled it. Some bloke called Pete Mundey wrote it after overhearing an old lady say that, old though she was, she still liked having her clock wound up now and again. What? How the hell do I know a song about sex in old age? Lennon and McCartney wrote "When I'm Sixtyfour" and maybe they set the trend, but how do I know the chorus, word for word. I told a friend of mine about my conundrum and he came up with a plausible explanation. He said, "You're not getting any younger Bill. Maybe the missus is playing the song whilst you're asleep, hoping it'll have a positive subliminal effect on your performance. Oh no …has she been talking?

OPEN FARMLAND ALL AROUND.

Not far out of Rugby is Hillmorton Locks, where we meet a lady getting ready to open the lock gates for her hubby. Why is it always the ladies doing the manual work whilst the men are at the helm playing "Captain"? Is that fair? I often share my observation with any lady crew who care to listen, and they either agree and moan about their downtrodden existence or accept that men are superior and laugh it off. She laughed. Aye aye, Capt'n.

It's very quiet today. No dog walkers, cyclists, runners or fishermen, and only one boat sailing. That's surprising considering there are more boats on the canals today than at the height of the Industrial Revolution. We're at least five miles out of town and another bridge dedicated to the worship of rugger comes into view. Sorry Frank, your invention may have revolutionised air travel the world over, but that's just not impressive enough for Rugby.

Just before Braunston (the only village on this trip) is a new marina and it looks well laid out and with an impressive new bridge. It's not often you see a new bridge on the canal these days. A little further on a church steeple creeps into view, poking the skyline. It must be Braunston, where the Oxford and Grand Union Canals meet. It's also the busiest place on the UK canal network but quiet today. Work on the Grand Union Canal commenced at the end of the 18th century with the objective of speeding up the route to London. It soon took most of the traffic and Braunston Junction became the most important hub for traffic between London, the Midlands and beyond and was haulier's heaven with companies like Pickfords based here. Modern materials of the day were used and a pair of cast iron bridges from our old friends at Horseley Ironworks gracefully connect the towpaths. Another interesting bridge here is the turnover or "Rover" bridge. It allows horses towing the boats to cross without the need to uncouple, and the rounded brickwork on top of the bridge helps avoid chafing of the ropes.

ROVER BRIDGE.

Robert Catesby, leader of the Gunpowder Plotters lived not far from here and it's thought they held one of their many meetings at the house. Cholera visited Braunston in 1834, travelling along the canal from London's East End, where it was rife. The first person to die was a lady who took in bed linen for washing from a boat from London. The disease soon spread and out of a population of 1,400, 70 people were infected and 19 died. Families once lived on the boats in appalling conditions, working long hours, seven days a week and with no education for their children. In protest, boatmen went on strike in 1923 and the canal network came to a near standstill, with between 50 and 60 boats blocking the canals at Braunston Junction. The Transport and General Workers Union (TGWU) supported the boatmen, negotiating with the company Fellows, Morton & Clayton. After 14 weeks, their negotiations proved unsuccessful and the boatmen returned to work.

VIEW OF BRAUNSTON FROM THE TOWPATH.

Continuing along the Oxford Canal, we come to a bridge where a pile of chunky planks is stored. The next bridge along is the same. These planks will be used to form a dam on each bridge, so that the water in between can be drained to enable repairs. On some bridges, usually where road access is, or was difficult, you will see a small door, which secures a storage area for the planks. You may also notice grooves built into either side of the canal wall, where the planks slot in. Talking about grooves, some bridges still bear the marks of the ropes once used to tow the boats. Wet towropes picked up grit and rubbed the stone, brickwork or iron of the bridge supports, creating grooves. Many bridges have been extended, as roads have become wider and you can often see two or three different types of stone, brick or concrete depending when the work was done. Some farm access bridges have only removeable poles and chain instead of walls, to allow wide loads to cross. And some look decidedly run-down, dangerous and in need of a little TLC.

THIS FARM BRIDGE NEEDS A LITTLE TLC

Along this section of the Oxford Canal you see well-groomed gardens where boats are moored. Some have sheds, greenhouses, trampolines, climbing frames and all the usual garden paraphernalia usually associated with a house. And there are a couple of massive barges here. There's no way they'll fit through the locks. Permanent homes I guess. The difference between a barge and a narrowboat is size. A narrowboat beam (width) is usually seven feet or less to guarantee easy passage through the canal network. Anything wider is technically a barge, although some of the old craft were built over seven feet and now have trouble getting through the locks due to movement on some lock walls. Length is important too with 72 feet (21.95 metres) being the maximum. Anything longer won't fit the locks. In the north, there are some locks at only 56 feet long and even 40 feet on the odd, isolated canal.

Walking past a couple of barges I notice a poorly looking

THE FERRETMAN.

pheasant in a cage and stop to check it out. It's not poorly at all, it's dead. Suddenly, it moves. I jump back in shock and two cheeky little ferret faces come up for air. Then "The Ferretman" appears and explains he collects roadkill to feed his jills (female ferrets). "Do you want to hold one?" ... Sure ... She's very soft and wriggly and doesn't bite. To keep them fit and entertained, he's built an amazing network of pipes connected to another cage. It's a Fun Park for Ferrets. He takes his ferrets and whippet hunting for rabbits. The jills go down the rabbit hole to flush them out and the whippet chases, catches and kills them. It's his sport. He used to let them run free on his boat, until his girlfriend complained. Spoilsport. The Ferretman is definitely the most interesting chap I've met along the canal for a while.

Another church steeple comes into view. It must be the tiny village of Lower Shuckburgh and the Church of St. John the Baptist in the Wilderness. Someone has built a nice little footbridge here to connect farm with church. It really is quiet here today so maybe time for a lesson in canal slang. How many words originating from the canal can you identify in this sentence?

"The gongoozler looked on as the toerag legged it down the cut, being chased by the navvy".

Let's start with the best... GONGOOZLER. Oh what a fantastic word. "Gongoozler" means someone who likes watching canal activity without getting involved.

"Toerag" ... Sometimes local boys would be paid to walk or "leg" the barge through a tunnel. They were poor kids, the lowest of the low in canal hierarchy and wore rags on their feet. And that's where "toerag" comes from.

"Legging it" was a term used to describe the job of "walking" a narrowboat through a tunnel where there is no towpath by lying on deck and "walking" on the tunnel ceiling and walls.

"Cut" ... The canal was not dug, it was cut and that is why the canal is known as the "cut".

"Navvy"... Unskilled workers, usually from Ireland, who came to England in the mid-1700s to navigate and dig out the canals were called "navvies".

There you have it. Some words in common use, some not and one ... G O N G O O Z L E R ... which ought to be.

LEGGING IT THROUGH THE TUNNEL

We've reached Napton Junction, also known as Wigram's Turn, named after long-time lock-keeper John Wiggenham. The village of Napton-on-the Hill is not far, with its 12th century church and 16th century windmill sitting on top of the hill. As the Oxford Canal continues south, we join the Grand Union Canal and soon come to Calcutt Locks also known as Wigram's Three. These are the first locks we've seen since Hillmorton early this morning, emphasising how flat the land is around here. This area is packed full of marinas which, in turn, are packed full of narrowboats moored up for the winter. This really does highlight how popular narrowboating is right now. From here, the canal starts the long drop westward down to Warwick where it crosses the River Avon.

Bridge 21. This is where we exit for Stockton and prepare for another 30-minute walk to the car. Coming up to road level, there's a nice looking pub right next to the bridge, and as I get my bearings I see what looks remarkably like a bus stop. How did that get here? It wasn't on the bus route map. Was it? My aching legs start cussing and swearing at me as they walk another 30 unnecessary minutes to find the car. Sorry legs.

What have I learnt today? Don't believe weather forecasts, a jill is a female ferret and I really do need more work on my bus travelling skills.

Six

HAWKESBURY TO COVENTRY

5.6 MILES

Bill Savage

Do you fancy going off-piste today? What about a walk into Coventry from Hawkesbury Junction? It's only a bendy five and a half miles and we'll see how the canal brought coal into the city to fuel the industrial machinery and power stations, enabling Coventry's entrepreneurial forefathers to do their thing.

I've arrived at Coventry bus station much too early for the bus to Hawkesbury. It's Sunday, the shops are closed and I can't find anywhere for a coffee. I usually do a bit of people-watching to pass the time but there's not much activity today, so I'll window shop instead. A wig shop catches my eye, only because the window display is so bad it's good. I've not got much hair so I contemplate which "rug" would suit me best. Then the bus arrives and, as I get on, a chap staggers off looking a little dazed and confused, still recovering from a heavy Saturday night I guess. He blinks, rubs his face down with both hands, gurns at me toothless and walks on. I think nothing of it until I find a pair of specs on the seat I'm about to sit on. The lady across the aisle tells me they belong to the dazed and confused man. The bus is already well on its way, so I hand them to the driver and then, just in case, check for false teeth before sitting down. The lady tells me she's off to church to pray 'cuz she's having an operation next week. It's her knee you see ... she's already had her hip done. And just like the Kind Lady I met on the Nuneaton bus that wasn't going to Nuneaton, she tells me in graphic detail about her past, present and future ailments. I try steering her away from some of the more personal details by telling her about my poorly toe. As soon as she hears the word "toe", I get full chapter and verse, not only about HER toes and feet, but also her mums, her aunts' and her sisters'. Apparently, feet run in the family (sorry, I know it sounds like a lame joke, but that's what she said, and not in a jokey way either). At last, I press the button for my stop and escape the torture. Why do random bus ladies like telling me all about their medical bits?

There was a difference of six inches in height between the Oxford and the Coventry canals and at Longford, a unique lock with one of the smallest rises/falls on the canal network joined them. Coal was discovered here in 1689 and it became an area of scattered pits. A gasworks, power station and large concrete factory making kerbstones, air-raid shelters and the like all resided along this section of the canal. We can see the Ricoh Arena from the towpath. It sits on what was the gasworks and is now home to Wasps Rugby Union Club and Coventry City Football Club.

Foleshill is next. George Eliot moved from Nuneaton (where we last met him ... I mean her) to Foleshill and her novel, "*Middlemarch*" is thought to be set around here but focuses on the rural, not the industrial aspect of the area. I've not read *Middlemarch* but judging by the historic records, Foleshill was one hell of a seedy place. I lifted these words from an 1840 report to Parliament. And I quote; "Lawlessness" ... "Immorality" ... "Drunkenness" ... "Poverty" ... "Depression" ... "Ignorance". The report ends "... the magistrates of Coventry well know that when a desperate case is brought before them it is generally from this neighbourhood." Criminality was also rife. A well-organised supply chain for silk nicked off the canal barges was established here by some clever Coventry villains. Watch out Peaky Blinders, you've got competition.

Next to the canal is the Courtaulds factory, where the world's first manmade fibres were produced, and over 5,000 people once worked here. It's now being converted into a housing estate. As the canal became busier, a privately owned railway was built to provide transport for Courtaulds and other local factories. Rover and Cammell-Laird are just two of the famous companies once based around here, taking advantage of cheap fuel supplies and transport.

Budding graffiti artists have been busy. A long stretch of corrugated steel fencing provides a wavy canvas for their work. What's it hiding? Probably another derelict factory site. Opposite is a new housing estate in the process of being built. I'm sure it was old workshops and warehouses the last time I came by. A little further on there's more graffiti and another derelict factory. This one has a chimney with a tree growing out of its spout. It feels like I've stepped into a spaghetti

FACTORY READY
FOR DEMOLITION.

western with tumbleweed rolling down the deserted street as a cheroot munching Clint Eastwood emerges from a rundown bar. By the time I do this route again, it'll probably have been replaced with a housing estate. Waterfront properties are very popular around here. I shall return to take pictures before this industrial heritage is bulldozed and lost forever.

Just before we reach Stoke Heath Basin, we go through one of my favourite new tunnels, covered in graffiti and with good lighting at one end to produce some excellent reflections in the water. This area would have been a hive of activity as soon as the canal opened back in 1769. Clay and sand were excavated close by, with a brick factory not too far away. As the Industrial Revolution took hold, various forms of metal-bashing blossomed and workshops popped up all around this area.

THE NEW STOKE HEATH TUNNEL

The focus of attention changed with the approach of the First World War and munitions became the order of the day, bringing unprecedented wealth to Coventry. As industry rapidly expanded, more factories were built along the canal, forming a pipeline to move raw materials in and finished goods out of Coventry. Bicycle manufacture occupied around 100 workshops and later motorcycle manufacture added another 140'ish. In 1896 Britain's motor industry was born when the first Coventry Daimler automobile emerged from a disused mill, the first car factory in Britain. Eventually, over 130 motor vehicle producers set up shop in Coventry and by 1955, Britain was the second largest manufacturer of cars in the world. At that time, 90% of production came from just five companies (BMC, Standard-Triumph, Ford, Vauxhall and Rootes) and Coventry was home to three of them. Two significant others based in Coventry were Jaguar and Rover (two separate companies at the time). The city would also have been teeming with other businesses to support this thriving industry with the canal working flat out just to keep up. Imagine the cacophonous industrial noises of grinding metal and thumping machinery. Metallic, nauseating smells, stinging eyes and invading nostrils. Filthy smoke and soot staining everything, creating dense smog to blanket the city in noxious fumes and limiting visibility to just a few feet. Cough or blow your nose and your hanky stains black. We sure have come a long way since those days.

Alongside the factories, homes were also needed for the ever-expanding workforce and roads full of old terraced houses surround the area. The old houses now share their neighbourhoods with blocks of new homes, built where workshops, warehouses and factories once stood. We're almost at Coventry Canal Basin as we pass Joseph Cash's 100 Houses. Joseph was a Quaker and successful businessman. He planned to build 100 homes, complete with power-driven looms on the top floor, to help home-working ribbon weavers compete with the new, mechanised factories.

VIEW FROM TOWPATH OF A TERRACED STREET

JOSEPH CASH'S
100 HOUSES

It was a model factory in the 1850's but only 48 were ever built, as the industry was taken over by cheap imports. It's nice to see these solid old buildings still standing and being used as Joseph intended – as homes.

We're almost at the end of the walk and pass some modern, impressive looking, waterside residential properties with a fancy new footbridge connecting both sides of the canal. Opposite is the site of the Daimler Works and only the Powerhouse building survives. The area has had some TLC applied and it's looking really smart and trendy (for Coventry). All that's needed now are a few upmarket bars, clubs and restaurants to mirror what Birmingham has done with its canal basins. Let's wait and see.

Bridge number one, just before Coventry's canal basin, is tiny, with no towpath running along the canal side. It was designed to be easily closed each evening with a wooden beam to keep the basin secure, and at one time, no boats were allowed to stay overnight. Now we're at the basin, I've found a great position to take a picture or two of the canal, with the old cathedral spire in the distance. It's a quiet, cosy little area with a few benches and judging by the litter, used extensively by drunks. There's a bloke leaning against the railings with a grey beard, looking not so much unshaven as unshaveable. He starts advising me where in Coventry to take the best pictures and lists a few locations, which from memory (not personal experience) are cosy little corners just like this where drunks, druggies and dropouts hang out. Next, he guides me to an exact position to capture the best composition for this particular shot (he's right) and tells me, in glorious detail, how he takes selfies (I didn't realise they could be so complex). Then, out of nowhere, someone says ... "He takes some good pics mate." The voice came from one of the benches and I realise there's a bloke wearing an off the shoulder grubby brown coat lying on it ... "He knows his stuff." says the lying down bloke, as he grunts and carefully sits himself up whilst expertly lighting a nub-end, inhaling gratefully. They both look harmless enough, but just in case, I enthuse about the photography expert's amazing knowledge and wonderful skill and thank him for his invaluable advice. I've either overdone the praise or it's because it's a few days after Christmas and the season of goodwill, but I'm offered a can of something. "That's very kind of you, but no thanks, I'm driving." I tell them. The photography expert explains he's not from around here, he's from London. Then he whips out his phone and wants a selfie. Him, his mate and ME. Suddenly I've become his best friend. How did that happen? I reluctantly oblige but it's difficult getting all three of us in the shot, and after getting way too close to both of them, I ask him "What are you doing here?" ... meaning what are you doing in Coventry? "I always cum 'ere for a drink wiv me mates ... it's best spot in town." he tells me, bad beery breath almost knocking me over. I don't bother correcting him and as he takes another selfie and they crack open a couple of cans, I bid them Happy New Year and farewell. Maybe they think I've come here for a drink too, what with my now muddy clothing, beanie hat pulled down tight and scruffy rucksack on my back.

VIEW OF CATHEDRAL SPIRES FROM CANAL BASIN.

We can't visit Coventry without mentioning the war. Coventry's well-established manufacturing base was a legitimate target for the Luftwaffe. Unfortunately, homes were woven into the same streets as the shops and factories. On the night of 14th November 1940, Coventry experienced the single most concentrated attack on a British City in WW2. Codenamed Mondscheinsonate (Moonlight Sonata) by the enemy, 515

German bombers dropped 500 tons of high explosives, 30,000 incendiaries and 50 landmines, destroying over half of the city's housing stock and turning Daimler's 15 acre factory site into a raging inferno. Canal water was to be used as backup for fire defences but the canal was breached early on and emptied. Demolition crews had to be prevented from pulling down the leaning cathedral tower, they didn't realise it had been like that for at least 100 years. And at 295ft., it's the third tallest spire in England. The attack was well planned and well executed, targeting defences, infrastructure, manufacturing, monuments and more. Imagine, half of the homes on your street damaged or destroyed. Surviving the aftermath, let alone the attack would have been horrendous. And it's not surprising to find that some Coventrians wanted the country to surrender. The official death toll was 554 but many more people were unaccounted for. Only one enemy aircraft was brought down. Interestingly, on 25th August 1939, the IRA planted a bomb in Coventry in their support for the German cause. It resulted in 5 deaths and 70 injuries but was knocked off the headlines by the outbreak of World War 2. And, on 14th February 1984, a Coventry Police Inspector accidentally set off a Nuclear War Warning System, prompting a flood of hysterical calls to the police from frightened residents of Coventry and surrounding towns.

I lived and worked in Coventry for a short while, where the old urban areas are a mixture of terraced homes with a shop on every corner, workshops, pubs and the occasional row of shops with living quarters above. Where I lived, not too far from the canal, streets had unexpected spaces between buildings where property had been destroyed during the war. Looking down a terraced street today, you can often see where property has been rebuilt but just doesn't match the other houses. Or, there's an unplanned space for parking or a hand car wash somewhere along the street.

Coventry, City of Culture 2021. "What?! You've got to be joking!". That's what most people who don't know the city would say. Why does Coventry give off such bad vibes? It's modern but proud of its history, vibrant, multi-ethnic, has three cathedrals, two top flight universities, a brilliant indoor market and was voted third happiest university city in the UK. There is much more to say about today's Coventry, but let's leave that for now and get down and dirty with ten little known facts about this city of culture.

1. Two-tone music created by bands like The Specials, Madness and Selecter was born in Coventry. The song "*Ghost Town*" by the Specials describes Coventry in the early 1980s, reflecting the city's (and the country's) economic fall from grace.

2. Coventry had the first ethnic minority policeman in the UK in 1960.

3. City planners started the destruction of Coventry well before the Luftwaffe arrived. A journalist writing in the *Illustrated London News* in the 1920s described Coventry as the best-preserved medieval city in Europe. By 1931 city planners had bulldozed large sections of medieval Coventry to improve traffic flow. The Luftwaffe did the rest.

4. The British sports car once ruled the world and most were made in Coventry, including the Jaguar E type. It was described by Enzo Ferrari as "The most beautiful car in the world". Whilst on the subject, did you know that by the end of the 1930's, one in five Coventrians owned a car, something not achieved nationally until the 1960's. Coventry was booming.

5. During the 1450's, King Henry VI and Queen Margaret moved their seat of power from London to Coventry.

6. Mister Rock & Roll himself, Chuck Berry, recorded his number one hit 'My Ding-A-Ling' at The Locarno, a

Coventry dance hall where Pete Waterman was once D.J. It's probably Chuck's worst ever composition. No, it's definitely his worst composition.

7. In the 14th century, tax inspectors rated Coventry as the fourth wealthiest town in England.

8. Some people love it, some loathe it but the fact is that the first pedestrian shopping precinct in the whole of Europe was built in the centre of Coventry.

9. The term "Peeping Tom" originates from Coventry. Legend has it that Tom spied on Lady Godiva as she rode naked through the streets of the town and he was struck blind. The term "True Blue" originates from the azure blue dye which made Coventry famous during the Middle Ages. Around 1640, the time of the Civil War in England, any Royalist soldiers captured in Birmingham were sent to Coventry for imprisonment - hence the term "Sent to Coventry".

10. Last and definitely not least, Frank Whittle of turbojet engine fame was born in Coventry.

I've never been able to work out how the life was sucked out of Britain's vibrant motor industry so quickly. Three years after Margaret Thatcher was elected Prime Minister, British Leyland employees dropped from 27,000 to 8,000. And then there were none. Management blame the unions and the unions blame management. Or was it political meddling? What's the true story? It's always baffled me so I'm off to Coventry Transport Museum to try and join up the dots.

There is a section in the museum about strike action, loss of jobs and eventual closure of factories. The story is mainly told with images of newspaper headlines of the time with their own propaganda bias. I remain baffled and no further forward. Anyway, Coventry Transport Museum is brilliant (and free). I came away awestruck by the sheer ingenuity, enterprise and imagination of our motor industry giants as they took the newly invented internal combustion engine and created their own versions of the motorcar. And the motorbike, and bus, and tractor, and lorry, and tank, and, and, and ... Plus, an array of add-ons, some still used today, to improve every aspect of motoring and the motor vehicle.

Standing proudly in front of Coventry Transport Museum is a large statue of ... (fanfare please) ... Air Commodore Sir Frank

Whittle OM, KBE, CB, FRS, FRAeS, inventor of the turbojet engine. Today, there's a kids' funfair behind Frank and it looks like Jiminy Cricket is taking the Micky. Sorry Frank. Anyway, at last … Justice for Frank. Well-done Coventry.

THE FRANK WHITTLE STATUE.

Seven

Stockton to Shrewley

17 miles

Bill Savage

We had heavy snow on Sunday. It's now Thursday and most of the main roads are clear, with only the lanes remaining affected. The plan is to walk from Stockton to Warwick today, around 11 miles. Things don't go to plan though, and you may witness a grown man cry.

Our bus is seven minutes late and the bus queue is turning nasty, full of very grumpy people cussing to themselves. I feel I ought to join in, but I'm enjoying the experience in a perverse sort of way. The bus drops me off where I should have parked the car the last time and we're soon on our way. Crikey, it's cold and walking on ice is going to slow us down, so let's try running. With only a few stumbles between patches of solid ground, it's haphazard but surprisingly successful, and it's keeping me warm. After running for a while, something catches my eye, so I stop to take a better look. It's a snow-covered field full of orange dots. Strange fruit? They're pumpkins. I wonder if they're still edible? After finding a way through the thick hedge and into the field I see that they're rotting. Getting out of the field isn't so easy. Oh, what a palaver. Eventually, I find my original footprints leading into the field and follow them out again to make my escape.

Stockton is a mainly Victorian village and the area was once dominated by the smoking chimneys of the cement works. Plenty of old quarries remain and looking out from the towpath today, only one chimneystack pokes the skyline. Huge fossils have been found in the blue lias clay around here, and cement from the old factories was used to build the Thames Embankment. The area has more than its fair share of old pubs and inns, built for the factory workers from the cement industry. Navvies and canal workers liked a drink and most of the pubs all along the Warwick Ring were built for them and are a wonderful legacy.

If you've stayed with me this far into the trip, you should know me by now so I'll share this with you. (If you're of a nervous disposition, look away now.) I'm a regular kind of a guy, but not in a Tony Blair kind of way. Hitting the road before the poo fairy paid me a visit this morning was a little foolish. I've got a feeling I'm still on her list. Oh, well, it must be done. Thank goodness I picked up a newspaper this morning and whoever invented wet wipes deserves a big statue, or at least a gold medal.

Not far from here is Long Itchington, which was 20 times bigger than Birmingham when the Doomesday Book was written. Almost 1,000 years later the census of 2011 records a population of 2013 with Birmingham at 1,073,045. Here's an interesting story and a world first. In 1949, an aircraft nicknamed the "Flying Wing" crashed with the pilot, one J.O. Lancaster, floating down, suspended by his parachute, onto a farm in Long Itchington. The aircraft, an AW52 built by Armstrong Whitworth of Coventry was experimental and jet engined. More significantly, this was the first time an ejector seat had been used in a flight emergency anywhere in the world. It was designed and manufactured by Martin-Baker Aircraft Company, which is still run by the same family.

ARMSTRONG WHITWORTH AW52 FLYING WING

Since then, it's reckoned over 7,500 lives have been saved by ejector seats. Another minor historical fact is that Queen-Liz-the-first once stayed here.

A man's voice from a boat in a lock says "G'day mate". Sounds Australian? "Good morning" say I in my best English accent. The voice belongs to one of the blokes out of ZZ Top. I didn't know ZZ Top were Australian. It's not ZZ Top of course, he just looks like one of them. It's Rob from Adelaide on holiday with his family. After a short chat, I head on, leaving Katrina, Kate, Leah and Josh shivering on the canal bank and I'm thinking ... Why? Why here? Why now? No one in their right mind has a two-week holiday on a canal in England in the middle of winter. On my phone, I check the weather in Adelaide and today it's 25°C and sunny. Tomorrow, 27°C and a little overcast. What are you doing, torturing your family like this Rob? I know where I'd rather be. Listen Rob ... you're bloody crazy mate. G'day.

The Warwick Ring cuts across a couple of Roman roads. We're now passing under the Fosse Way again, which links Exeter with Lincoln. The other is Watling Street which links Dover to Holyhead on Anglesey. The Romans built a few canals in Britain too, mainly for drainage, irrigation or to connect two navigable rivers. One of them, Foss Dyke on the River Trent, is still in use to this day. That's pretty impressive. Imagine if some of our canals are still in use in two thousand year's time. I do hope so.

I've seen the occasional tent or sleeping bag or cardboard mattress around Birmingham canal towpaths, but never anything like this little encampment with its tents and covered, open-plan living/cooking area. It's well hidden amongst the trees, with a small gap through the hedge and a path leading to two tents. "Hello, is anyone home?" Best to check before shooting any pictures. It feels like I'm intruding, encroaching into someone's privacy, stepping uninvited into their home. Wow, it looks tidy and quite homely. Clothes on the line, mirror above a double washbasin (two plastic tubs), cooking pots, running water (they're camped next to a fast-flowing stream). There are no empty beer cans or other alcohol litter. That's a good sign. I'm leaving a note pinned to a tree asking if someone could give me a call so that I can put their story into this book. Slim chance, I know, but it could be interesting.

We're passing the old Flavel factory, so we must be in Leamington Spa, recently voted the happiest town in Britain. Really? How do you measure happiness? Count smiley faces per square kilometre? Leamington would definitely win my vote for town with the most cafés. There are loads and new ones popping up everywhere. Could this be why everyone here is so happy? The Flavel factory was built in 1833, next to the canal to take advantage of improved transportation. Eventually, it occupied 40% of the town and Flavel became the biggest manufacturer in the world of kitchen appliances. Their first product, in the mid-17th century, was gunpowder and it made the company very wealthy due to the many wars and campaigns being waged at the time. Later, their main line became cooking appliances, but they always supported the war effort, with cannon balls for Trafalgar and Waterloo, and various other munitions and armoury until the end of WW2. Now, the company specialises in gas fires and is still British owned.

Four swans are floating around doing nothing in particular. Swans are supposed to be photogenic, so I pull out the camera and get ready for the perfect shot. It's a scruffy area and there's not much swan action so I put it away and walk on. A few seconds later I hear a loud, deep thumping sound from behind. As I turn to see what was happening, my flabber has never been so gasted by the amazing spectacle of four swans taking off, already in V formation, just a few feet above my head. Their sheer size and the feeling of power from their wings as they whoooosh overhead is incredible. Then, to my surprise, they land just a few metres ahead and join a gaggle of ducks being fed by a lady and her little boy. The experience was mesmerising. So mesmerising, in fact, I didn't even think to get the camera out and it was over in the blink of an eye. The experience was enough for me. Truly magnificent.

A plaque next to Bridge 40 lists a few Leamington Spa historical people and local facts. I see that Queen Victoria's first overnight stay was here, in 1830 when she was only 11 years old. That's why it's called ROYAL Leamington Spa. But there is no mention of Napoleon III who once lived here. Or that the first Lawn Tennis Club in the world was formed here, and elephants were regularly washed on the riverbanks in town (what?). Frank Whittle pops up again. He lived, went to school and worked in Leamington. The undisputed Middleweight Champion of the World was born here, too. Randolph Turpin (fight name The Leamington Licker) was a very talented boxer of mixed race, but not very good with money. In 1966, at the age of 37, he put a pistol to his head and pulled the trigger. It's the sort of sad story a young Bob Dylan would sing about before he went electric. I notice Terry Frost has a very large area dedicated to his life next to the bridge. Terry who? ... No, me neither. Apparently, he was an abstract artist born in Leamington Spa.

It's amazing how quickly things change. I've been doing this route for the last four years and each year something old and familiar turns into, usually, new waterside homes. This time it's a few old Leamington canal-side workshops now replaced by two large, very smart student accommodation blocks. Not quite new homes, but almost. Leamington Spa was originally known as Leamington Priors until about 1800 when the small village rediscovered its saline springs and started building baths around them. In July 1814 The Royal Pump Rooms were officially opened, offering spa treatment claiming to cure or relieve a huge number of disorders. The town became very fashionable with the rich and famous and, like other spa towns in England, it brought great wealth to Leamington. In 1851 only four people were registered as unemployed out of a population of 16,000. But this was soon to change as the fashion for "Taking the Waters" declined and the pump rooms started to experience hard times. Today, they form the nucleus for a museum, art gallery, library and café, only a seven minute walk from the canal. Well worth a visit.

Heading for Warwick, first we cross an aqueduct over the main railway line to London, then proceed across another aqueduct over the River Avon. Here, the river forks with the Avon travelling southwest and a new river, the Leam travelling east. Walking over the river aqueduct offers another example of how nothing stood in the way of my canal hero, the 18th and 19th century navvy.

Most towns we have travelled through have an enterprise they call their own. Remember Fazeley red tape, Nuneaton coal, Atherstone hats, Rugby, well … rugby, Stockton cement and Leamington and its spa. What does Warwick have? History, and bucket-loads of it. Warwick Castle, on the banks of the River Avon, was founded on the order of William the Conqueror in 1068 and is now one of the best examples of a medieval castle anywhere in Britain. In 1694, the Great Fire of Warwick destroyed much of the centre of town although there remain good examples of medieval buildings, including the superb, higgledy-piggledy Lord Leycester Hospital next to the equally impressive West Gate. These buildings have been used in many historically-set television productions. We could be heading for a major history overload here so that's enough. If you want to know more about Warwick, come visit. Most people only see the castle and never venture into town. Don't you make that mistake.

We're just passing The Cape of Good Hope pub and it's always very difficult to walk past without popping in for a pint and a chat with New Zealander, Narrowboater and Landlord,

Steve. The pub was built in 1799, specifically for canal workers, and Steve is a font of knowledge (his beer isn't bad either). Motor racing legend and sports car designer/builder, Donald Healey, regularly used the pub. His factory was very close to the canal, as was the Triumph Motorcycle Works after their main Coventry factory was destroyed by the Luftwaffe in 1940. Warwick Prison was just up the road and Steve has plenty of interesting stories from that era. The pub is interesting and full of history, with its frontage facing the canal. Roadside, you wouldn't know it was there. That's why it's called "Warwick's Best Kept Secret".

We've arrived at Saltisford Wharf in Warwick, which was where the Warwick and Birmingham Canal terminated. It lay derelict and unloved for many years and was in danger of being filled in for redevelopment. When local man, Dick Amende was made unemployed in 1982, he decided to help others in the same predicament by bringing them together to save the area. The unemployed were used in a similar way in the 1930s when the Grand Union locks were widened. Money, materials and equipment were donated or loaned, and the Saltisford Canal Trust charity was formed with the area being officially opened in 1985.

The plan was to exit at Warwick but I'm thinking of continuing to Hatton Locks and the café to buy a new map. The old one is falling to bits. We've been travelling downhill since lock no.1 at Calcutt. The first uphill lock we come to is lock no.23 at Radford Semele then, after Warwick we climb towards the famous Hatton Flight of 21 locks. I didn't realise how low-lying this area is, but it's no surprise with the River Avon running through the middle of Warwick. The view of Warwick and the Church of St. Mary from Hatton top lock is stunning. It's getting late and by the time we reach the café, it's shut. Oh, well, what now? Home is not too far. I could make a phone call and ask for a lift, but a lift means I've failed in my challenge. Let's walk.

HATTON FLIGHT OF LOCKS ON A HAZY WINTER'S MORNING

117

Today, the canal has been mostly frozen. In the old days, when the canal iced over, employees were put on half pay whilst the self-employed received nothing, so it was in everyone's interest to keep the waterways workable. If the ice was not too thick, iron iceboats pulled by four horses were used to clear a path. It's always amusing to watch ducks and geese plodding around on the ice, not knowing quite what has happened to their world. Dogs are funny too, skidding along, chasing the ducks. The most surreal thing I've seen are heavy objects like bricks dropped onto the ice. They appear to be floating and stick out at all angles as the ice starts to thaw.

Past Hatton it's much colder and the towpath is icy, uneven and very slippy and I'm glad to reach Shrewley Tunnel. We exit here. Home is only two miles away. It's dark now and walking the icy lanes proves eventful but I don't get run over and slip over only once. At last, home, and after over 17 hard miles I'm cold, I'm tired, my legs ache, my feet hurt, I'm hungry, I'm thirsty and I need a pee. As I arrive at the door of my dark house, I realise there is no one in. Then it dawns on me, I left the house key in the car which I parked miles away this morning in Leamington. Self-pity and self-loathing should only be performed in private, so I'm going around the back of the house to find somewhere to curl up and die. But first, I need a pee. Ah, what's this …? The shed door is unlocked. As I'm getting comfortable on a couple of old tyres, I recognise some dusty bottles at the back of a shelf. It's that disgusting wine I made a few years back, put away to "age" in the hope it would become a little closer to "drinkable". In the circumstances, it's absolutely delicious. Living the Dream. Cheers!

Well, what a surprise. About five weeks after leaving the note on the tree, I got a phone call from a friend of the people who live at the canal encampment. The call was to check me out and make sure I was kosher. I find out it's a couple who live at the "camp", Grzegorz and Marta from Olsztyn in Poland. We arrange to meet at a "happy café" in Leamington Spa and I'm really looking forward to finding out their story.

Grzegorz, I'll call him Greg from now on, and Marta, are in their late twenties to early thirties, casually dressed and not what you'd expect tent dwellers to look like. They came to the UK around two years ago and have lived at the camp for much of that time. Greg is a carpenter by trade and Marta a cook, and their work is erratic, so money is always a worry. Most of the time, living at the camp is okay, especially during the summer months. But winters are cold and wet. Very wet. The recent heavy snow collapsed one of their tents and the storms have brought down branches, but they survive. I ask if they feel safe and yes, they do. But they were attacked one time by a couple of crazy racists who wanted them to "go home". One had an iron bar, and the other, some kind of blowlamp pointed at Marta's head. Luckily the thug's lighter didn't work. Greg is well built and looks as though he can handle himself and he managed to fight them off. They share their camp with a rat catching cat who thinks it's a dog. They found it as a kitten and it'll chase away anything or anybody that comes near. A "Beware of the Cat" sign wouldn't go amiss. Cooking is done over an open fire and Marta's cooking skills come in handy. After a meal, they will sit around the fire with the cat and a family of four swans will regularly join them. Sometimes ducks too. Their morning wakeup call is from a family of seven ducks who peck at Greg through the tent canvas to remind him it's breakfast time. Although Greg and Marta say living at the camp is okay, they know that eventually they will need permanent accommodation. It all relies on work and so far the agency they use has offered only temporary jobs, so they will visit the library every morning and use the computers there to continue searching. Before we part company, I tell them I will call into the camp the next time I pass and leave a gift. Maybe something Polish? I ask Greg if he drinks beer and he gives me the kind of look that says ..."Is the Pope Catholic? Of course I drink beer, I'm Polish." His favourite is Tyskie beer and he likes kielbasa sausage, too. Then Marta invites me to join them for a meal sometime. I'll be keeping in touch and look forward to joining Greg, Marta, four swans, seven ducks and a crazy cat for dinner.

Good luck Marta and Greg and I hope you find what you're looking for real soon.

EIGHT

SHREWLEY TO BIRMINGHAM

18 MILES

Bill Savage

We're at Shrewley Tunnel again, the start of the next leg of our walk. Built in 1798, it's 396 metres long and has no towpath, but it does have the unique feature of a horse tunnel. If we were travelling by barge in the old days, we'd unhitch our horse and lead it up the path, through the horse tunnel, over the hill and down the other side to re-join the canal. And we'd pay a penny to a toerag to "leg" the barge

SHREWLEY TUNNEL WITH HORSE TUNNEL ON RIGHT.

through to the other side. The main London Marylebone railway line was laid down around 1896 and cuts straight through the same hill as the tunnel. During the 1990s, the M40 motorway was extended to join the M42 near Birmingham and guess what? It cuts straight through the same hill as the canal and railway. It's early, it's foggy, it's just starting to get light and the plan is to walk to Birmingham, around 18 miles away.

After we exit the tunnel, we walk through Shrewley Cutting, which is now a site of special interest due to the rock formations from the Triassic age. We soon reach Rowington and the very interesting looking Tom O' The Wood pub, which was once a windmill. There were another two windmills around here, the Grinning Jenny and Bouncing Bess. Catherine Parr, the sixth wife of King Henry VIII owned the local manor and not far is Shakespeare Hall, reputed to have been the home to a branch of William Shakespeare's family. It's thought to be where he wrote, "*As You Like It*". Now we meet a fisherman sitting quietly on the bank. The scene looks good, with him hunched over his rod and the light shining through the morning mist as a backdrop, so I ask if he minds me taking his picture. What I didn't expect was for him to carefully put down his rod, stand up and strike a camp pose … one hand on hip, one finger on lips ... an "I'm yours if you want me" kind of cheeky smile … the whole nine yards. AHHHH! … One hell of a freaky moment so early in the morning but entertaining too. I think he's trying to embarrass me for some reason so, to avoid encouragement (he doesn't need it), I don't take his photo. Instead, I explain about the mist and morning light. He looks a little disappointed. Once he's sitting down again, with rod in hand (no, that's not a euphemism), I take the picture, thank him and quickly walk on. I wish I'd taken the posing picture now.

Baddesley Clinton is a 13th century, moated manor house situated in Lapworth, the next village along. Featured in the very first scene of the TV series *"Gunpowder"*, the manor house has three priest holes and was used as a Catholic safe house in the 16th century. Two people from the house were tortured and killed for helping Catholic priests and the manor played a pivotal role in the plot to blow up parliament.

The Stratford upon Avon Canal and the Grand Union Canal meet here at Kingswood Junction. The Warwick Ring follows the Grand Union Canal north into Birmingham. The Stratford Canal travels from Stratford upon Avon to join the Worcester Canal, which continues into Birmingham. Today we're following the Grand Union route.

We've already passed a surprising number of good-looking pubs since Hatton Locks, including the interestingly named "Black Boy". The name derives from the nickname of King Charles II, coined by his mother due to the darkness of his skin and eyes. We continue past another pub, bypassing the village of Knowle and on to Catherine-de-Barnes, a hamlet of the town of Solihull. The canal passes under the M42 motorway and crosses the River Blyth on a small aqueduct. Once a small farming community, Solihull began to grow as people moved out of Birmingham to escape the industrial grime. Brummies think anyone from Solihull is ever so posh, and people from Solihull agree and refuse to be associated with Birmingham. The town was recently named 2nd best place to live in the UK.

Other than the lone fisherman earlier on, the towpath is quiet, except for wildlife. Within the last few hundred yards we've passed a squirrel, a floating dead sheep, a rat, a lady duck being chased by four lusty man ducks, a dead fish, a heron, a family of swans and two more man ducks having a face off and then a fight over one lady duck (lucky girl). Now, about this heron. I've either seen four herons in the last couple of miles or one heron four times. Each time I try taking a picture, creeping closer and closer, but before I can say "Kodachrome" the bloody thing silently, gracefully and majestically glides away, glancing backwards, flashing me a mocking smirk. If only I had a gun.

Solihull is also home to The Rover Motor Company, now Jaguar Land Rover. A shadow factory built close to the canal in Solihull to support the war effort was "donated" to Rover when war came to an end. Steel was rationed and in very short supply at the time, severely affecting the ability to build new cars. However, aluminium was plentiful and the idea of a four-wheel drive, utilitarian vehicle requiring very little steel or tooling and cheap to build came to fruition. The Land Rover was born. That was in 1948 and although a stopgap measure at the time, around two million of this remarkable vehicle, in various guises, have been sold the world over. From farming to firefighting, Bob Marley to the Popemobile, it's a real British icon, just like the British Bobby or red telephone box. So, after almost 70 years of continuous production and healthy sales, the last Land Rover rolled off the production line on 29th January 2016. Mercedes and Toyota must be delighted as their Land Rover lookalikes fill the void.

We're now in the suburbs of Birmingham. Olton, to be exact and Hobs Moat isn't far. "Hob" is a medieval word meaning "hobgoblin" and it was thought the area possessed mysterious powers. It's certainly very quiet along this route as we walk ever closer to Birmingham City. Birmingham Airport isn't far, but I hear no jet engines. We've been walking for almost four hours and have not seen a soul, except for the fisherman. A large fallen branch, probably caused by the recent storm, blocks the towpath, but I manage to clamber over it. Two lads on bikes, a dog and its walker, a bloke in a canoe, a runner and another walker all pass by in quick succession. I try telling them about the branch, but they all seem in a bit of a hurry. Further on, on the other side of the canal I notice a hunched, hooded girl, sitting quietly, alone on a bench in a secluded copse, gazing intently at something in her hands. She appears mesmerised but suddenly starts stroking whatever is in her hand. Then she pokes and tickles it. Is she a Hobgobliness conjuring up mischievous spells from whatever creature is in her grasp? Is this why everyone is deserting this place? And what about all those creatures earlier on, including the dead sheep and dead fish? She stops the stroking, poking and tickling, puts one hand to her ear, stands up and walks on, occasionally talking and giggling to herself, perhaps laughing at her own wicked spells. Very, very mysterious. Let's get out of here.

It's interesting to look at crimes committed around the Warwick Ring in the late 19th century. Stabbings were plentiful and theft of cargo was very common but so was theft of horse or mule and even dog. Theft of a boy though? That's extreme. Here is a very small sample of some of the court cases from 1882.

Joseph Thay (alias Thirza) a canal boatman from Birmingham was charged with stealing a boy under the age of 10 years for the purpose of minding his horse. He invited the boy onto his boat for a ride and would not let him off. This was December 1882 and the boy spent the first night sleeping in a hedge in the rain. Although wet through, he kept his clothes on and the second night slept in a stable. This continued for about a week, sleeping outdoors and eating dry bread and boiled turnips. Whilst "Thirza" was at a house somewhere around Wolverhampton, the boy escaped. He walked the next two days along the canal to Derby. "Thirza" alleged that the boy refused to go home and the jury acquitted him.

James Walker, a boatman, was sent to jail for a month for cruelty to a horse. The animal had been forced to pull the barge for 48 hours without food or rest.

John Compton (22), a boatman, was fined 32s 6d (£1.62) for wasting water, the property of the Birmingham Canal Company. He wasted "sufficient to fill three locks".

John Fletcher, a boatman, was fined £1 1s 6d (£1.07) for cruelty to a mule. The defendant was seen at Hatton Locks striking the animal with an iron windlass, inflicting twelve blows.

Mary Ann Ross (21) was charged with stealing £28 10s from boatman George Jones whilst he was in Leamington and "in a house of ill fame". She was sentenced to four months imprisonment with hard labour.

As the canal flows over the River Cole, we pass Ackers Adventure Centre. Just two miles from the city centre and set in 75 acres of diverse landscape, it offers activities such as skiing, wall climbing, bush-craft survival, canoeing, kayaking, team building and loads more. It's a little gem amongst all this industrial grunge and grime. We're starting to see some serious graffiti so the city centre can't be too far away. The convenience of the canal makes it a major contributor to network gas pipes and electric, telephone and fibre optic cables. We've passed quite a few substations today and the gas markers have all been individually decorated by local graffiti artists. Bless 'em. You often see piles of litter around these markers. Litter does my head in. Crisp packets can take 75-80 years to decompose. Aluminium cans 200 years. Plastic bottles 500 years. Well done to the people who put up signs on the towpath, tackling the problem in different ways. I'm not sure these litter loving layabouts will take any notice though?

A COUPLE OF INTERESTING ATTEMPTS AT STOPPING PEOPLE LITTERING.

On this side of the canal, from Small Heath Bridge, the buildings have already been bulldozed flat, getting ready for HS2 and the next chapter in Birmingham's rich history.

SMALL HEATH BRIDGE AS SEEN FROM THE TOW PATH.

Armoury Road runs parallel to the canal and it's here that the Birmingham Small Arms Company once stood. We'll take a quick diversion off the towpath to see the famous factory building. BSA (as it became known) started life as a conglomerate of 14 Birmingham gunmakers and was set up in 1860 at the request of the government to mechanise gun making and keep pace with conflicts around the world. Until then, all guns were hand-built, unique, and impossible to maintain in the field of battle. A few BSA killing machines include the Lewis gun from WW1 and the Lee-Enfield from WW2, the Sten gun and the Browning machine gun, used in the Battle of Britain Spitfires and Hurricanes. War was very profitable, and the company grew to become an industrial giant, diversifying into anything and everything including bicycles, motorcycles, cars, buses and much more. They were once the largest motorcycle manufacturer in the world and even took over Daimler in Coventry for a while. The company ceased trading in 1973. However, an airgun manufacturer and dealer continue on the factory site, keeping the famous BSA name alive.

ONE SMALL CORNER OF THE BSA FACTORY

As we pass under one of the main railway lines in and out of Birmingham, the bridge arches have been taken over by small, motor trade businesses. Holy Trinity Church, a well-known landmark is in clear view and rough sleepers often frequent this area when the weather allows. A convenient, large'ish grassy bank is situated just before the canal disappears into the bowels of the city. This is where small, one-man tents are erected when the weather is a little kinder. Only two remain today and one of those is a burnt-out shell.

HOLY TRINITY CHURCH & A STRANGER SITTING ON THE LOCK.

There are all sorts of cosy corners under the streets at canal level for the homeless and rough sleepers to get some rest. But today it's winter and it's cold and it's deserted. Currently, Birmingham is in first place in the region for the number of homeless. Coventry is second and Rugby third. Here's another interesting statistic, Birmingham has 2.1 rough sleepers per 10,000 population, compared with 5.7 for Manchester and 189.6 for City of London.

THERE ARE PLACES FOR ROUGH SLEEPERS TO TAKE SHELTER.

We're approaching Bordesley Junction and a familiar looking bridge (Horseley Ironworks) where the canal forks. We're going straight on into the heart of the city. The other route would take us to Spaghetti Junction. It passes through an old industrial area of the city, once the Peaky Blinder's territory. Definitely worth a visit, but no off-piste today, my legs won't take it. Instead, we pass through Deritend, another old industrial district. Some say the name derives from "dirty end", because it was certainly a dirty place back in the day. In 1807, the English poet Robert Southey wrote about the area as if he was a Spanish nobleman:

"The noise of Birmingham is beyond description; the hammers seem never to be at rest. The filth is sickening: filthy as some of our own towns may be, their dirt is inoffensive; it lies in idle heaps, which annoy none but those who walk within the little reach of their effluvia. But here it is active and moving, a living principle of mischief, which fills the whole atmosphere and penetrates everywhere, spotting and staining everything, and getting into the pores and nostrils. I feel as if my throat wanted sweeping like an English chimney."

BORDESLEY JUNCTION

Although the canal was widened in the 19th century, many Birmingham city locks remain the old, narrow type. This was to preserve water and save money in constructing the 10 reservoirs necessary to operate a wider canal system in the city. Imagine the congestion. Many locks on the Warwick Ring were widened or else another lock was built next to the original, easing congestion, speeding things up and helping to compete with the railways. I've always had this nostalgic idea that locks work on old world charm and gravity. The other day, I saw a bloke wearing hi-vis disappear into one of the many little huts you see along the towpath. I asked him if I could have a look inside. It was like walking into the TARDIS. An array of lights blinking next to all manner of switches and knobs. No grease or grime or oily rags, just a gleaming, state-of-the-art control panel, all for one remote lock. Blimey.

The spectacular success of Britain's Industrial Revolution is in no doubt. It's a crying shame that so much wealth was created out of war and conflict, especially during a time when Britain was in the driving seat of world affairs. After all, you often hear boasts about how much of a world atlas was coloured pink, depicting British rule and British Empire. So much effort and creativity has been and still is exerted to perfect methods and machinery for killing our fellow humans. The ejector seat and jet engine, which we learned about earlier, were both conceived because of a wartime need. Our wars helped to create personal fortunes, commercial empires and a decent standard of living for many working people, with the evidence popping up all around the Warwick Ring.

As we walk ever closer to the heart of the city, I'm wondering when these old warehouse and workshop sites will be pulled down and disappear forever. You see the occasional fluorescent light blinking through a grimy window, but the area is sure to be replaced with modern commercial buildings or swanky waterside residential property soon. Walking through the art gallery that is Birmingham's prolific canal graffiti, the Rotunda and Selfridges buildings come into view and here the canal splits. Left are steps up to street level and a short walk to Moor Street Station for a comfortable ride home. Or right, a 50-minute walk past Aston University to Gas Street Basin and then another 15-minute walk to catch the train. No competition. Left it is then. As we reach street level and cross the road, we can look from the bridge to the Typhoo Basin and the old Typhoo Tea factory. Access by canal and towpath is blocked, and there are plans for redevelopment around here. I do worry that the area will be raised to the ground, with no respect or sympathy for these historic buildings. However, it's encouraging to see plans to bring back to life at least one of the historic canal premises. I was fortunate enough to be invited on a tour of the grade II listed Canal Office, and although this impressive, 19th century building has not been used since suffering fire damage back in 2004, it is solid, well-constructed and reasonably dry. As well as being a canal office, it's done time for Pickford's Carrying Company, a confectioner, metal works, brewery, coal merchant, screw manufacturer, sandwich shop and boxing club, plus various other enterprises I'm sure. Now, there are plans to transform the building into a permanent, affordable base for the fast-growing artistic community in the area and create a gallery where you can experience some of the most interesting contemporary art in the UK today. Looking at the building from the inside, with so much natural light streaming through the many large windows on three of the four

THE CANAL OFFICE

walls, I can see it becoming a fantastic exhibition space, art gallery and studios, plus the obligatory cafe. Bring it on …

VIEW FROM INSIDE CANAL OFFICE

That's it. We've just finished the Warwick Ring Canal Walk. But I'm not letting you escape that easily. There are a couple of off-piste excursions I'm planning, including the irresistible combination of Cadburys Chocolate and the Peaky Blinders drinking den. Please meet me in the next chapter.

MOOR STREET STATION WITH SELFRIDGES BEHIND.

NINE

DIGBETH BRANCH CANAL

5.6 MILES

Bill Savage

Some of the fake Brummie accents put me off when the popular TV series *Peaky Blinders* first came around in 2013. Last night, I watched the first, second and third episodes, a bit of a marathon I know - but it got me in the mood for today's walk into Peaky Blinder territory.

When I was a lad, my grandad used to talk "affectionately" about the Peaky Blinders and their razor blade hats. The TV series is set in the 1920s but in fact, the Peaky Blinders gang was at its peak in the late 19th century. Another gang called the Brummagem Boys took over and were kings of the heap before WW1. By the 1920s, the Brummagem Boys had morphed into The Birmingham Gang, who went on to become the most feared gang in the country. If you want to know more about the old gangs of Birmingham, get yourself a copy of Professor Carl Chinn's book, "*The Real Peaky Blinders*". It's fascinating.

We're starting the walk at Garrison Lane, only because it's mentioned so often in the TV series and I want to take a peek (pun intended) at where the gang operated from. The area

PEAKY BLINDERS TERRITORY

looks and feels no different to other Birmingham inner-city towpaths. Apart from one row of smart, modern residential buildings, the route is full of old factories, workshops and warehouses, many dilapidated and ready for the demolition gang. There are plenty of bridges, far more than on the other routes and there appears to be more old residential property around here. Talking of bridges, many around Birmingham have gates or doors set into the roadside parapet walls. They were put there for home defences during WW2 when, around 1852 tons of explosives and incendiaries were dropped on the city. Hoses could be lowered into the canal to pump up water for dousing flames and minimising damage, and they're still serviceable today.

BRIDGE WITH GATES FOR FIRE DEFENCE.

We're in Small Heath and as Birmingham's population expanded in the 18th and 19th centuries to cope with a booming economy, housing estates were laid out for the workers. The building land was full of clay pits and was advertised with the asset of clay for brick-making. These estates are literally made from the ground they sit on. St. Andrews Football Stadium, home to Birmingham City Football Club, was built on a clay pit not far from here. It was first set up in 1875 as the Small Heath Alliance Football Club.

A fisherman is comfortably ensconced by the next lock and I ask him if he's caught anything ... "Just missed a pike ... caught one last week ... 16 pounds ... caught one week before ... 32 pounds" ... I ask him if he's caught anything today. "Me and my Mate caught a whopper over there, it was ..." Oh, no, I fear another fisherman's tale brewing. At this rate his pike will soon be as big as a barge, so I bid him farewell and good fishing. I never really feel uneasy or threatened travelling the canal, even with the rich mixture of "characters" I meet along the way. But only a month ago, a couple of Peaky Blinder wannabes were caught robbing a fisherman and three walkers along this section of towpath. An 18 year old and a 16 year old were both charged with robbery, affray and carrying an offensive weapon. Maybe I've been lucky.

Yuk! What's that smell? As we leave the city, we come to a massive metal recycling plant. Taking a closer look, I see a flow of water gushing from its bowels and later find out it's the River Rea. No wonder the fish have sought shelter in the canal. The River Rea runs parallel to the canal for a while before joining the River Tame.

The overhead highways of Spaghetti Junction are up ahead and on the other side of the canal is Star City, the biggest leisure and entertainment complex in Europe when it opened in 2000. I've only ever seen it from the motorway and it looks a lot smaller close up. Unexpectedly, at ground level, sitting between the highways above is a lone house, not old and derelict but modern and occupied and looking so out of place. I wonder who lives there? The canal swings left now, under Spaghetti Junction to join the Birmingham and Fazeley Canal. Straight on and heading north is the Tame Valley Canal which takes you to the Black Country and beyond. Let's take a quick amble along the Tame Valley Canal and under the very dark motorway bridge/tunnel just a few yards up the towpath. In the centre of this dark expanse is a ventilation shaft which kindly lights up the far wall where we should find some of the best street art east of Digbeth. Oh dear, someone … probably the council … has painted the wall brown and obliterated any artistic efforts. Have you ever heard of Bill Drummond? He was a member of the band "Big In Japan"? In 1984 he created artwork along here, in exactly the same spot. He is the bloke who, in 1994, burned one million quid as a piece of art. Oh, what a selfish pillock. Just think of the worthy causes he could have given it to.

BILL DRUMMOND UNDER SPAGHETTI JUNCTION.

Back on the Birmingham and Fazeley Canal, there is the strange sight of a large internal wall looking very lonely on its own, the last remains of an old factory in the process of demolition. When we walked this route in an earlier chapter, the whole building was still there, in all its glory. It's amazing how quickly the view from the towpath changes.

Regularly walking the Warwick Ring, it's surprising what's still to be discovered. As we head back into the city, we go over many small bridges along here, where the canal has been blocked off and covered over. I've not noticed them before. They were built to cross the short canal spurs that fed the many factories, workshops and warehouses operating from this part of town.

CANAL SPUR BRIDGE ON B'HAM & FAZELEY CANAL.

After passing a lone narrowboat travelling through the locks towards the city, a familiar sight comes into view. It's another Horseley Ironworks Bridge and it's where the Birmingham and Fazeley Canal continues to Gas Street Basin. We will follow the route left, along the Digbeth Branch Canal, to meet the Grand Union and back to where we started.

A LONE NARROWBOAT TRAVELLING INTO THE CITY.

The Digbeth Branch Canal was completed in 1799 and was built to link the Grand Union Canal with Gas Street Basin. It's only 1.5 miles long and has very few old buildings now. There is one huge, old red brick building on the other side of the canal with its impressive chimneylike water tower dominating, sitting in the middle of a flat, empty landscape, surveying the battlefield which was once a thriving industrial district. It began life as a bed factory and offices for the CWS (Cooperative Wholesale Society). It has two entrances, one marked

"OFFICES" and the other "WORKERS and GOODS ENTRANCE". Office staff were not classed as "workers" in those days. Every time I walk past, it looks to be getting in a far worse state of repair. Security is usually pretty tight, but once, during the Tory conference season, when police and security were busy in another part of Birmingham, I managed to get through the security fence. Getting up close and personal with this majestic building just made me sad. It's falling to pieces with no attempt to preserve what's left.

WILL IT STAY OR WILL IT GO? DEMOLITION OR RENOVATION?

The modern, mostly university architecture along this route sits in stark contrast with the ancient tunnels and locks. Although they look a little out of place, they do remind us of

Birmingham's industrial past. Now, fast forward 100 years and what do you think will still be here? Modern university buildings? Or, old locks and tunnels?

As we pass through Ashted Tunnel and then Curzon Street Tunnel (now a listed building), the deafening rumble of trains is a reminder that the world's oldest railway terminus is somewhere above us. Curzon Street Railway Station opened in 1838 on a ten-acre site. It closed in 1966 and only the front facade remains. The whole area will soon be taken over by the new HS2 railway line and I now understand why so much of East Birmingham has been raised to the ground.

ASHTED TUNNEL

Oh yes, Curzon Tunnel. This is where I once thought I was going to be mugged. I was in Birmingham to attend a pesky "Speed Awareness Course" (it's better than points on your licence) and decided to take a shortcut along the towpath to get to the railway station for the train home. It was early evening, quite dark and as I entered the tunnel, a hooded figure appeared from the shadows. I thought he may be up to no good, so I changed my style of walking to imitate a gorilla and got ready to whack him with my manly man bag. No worries. My gorilla impersonation did the trick. It's a long tunnel, and halfway along I saw another hooded figure lurking around. Oh no. It looks like they're working together and I'm about to be "sandwiched" and robbed by these two thugs. I carried on walking, gorilla style, and got ready with the bag. Nothing happened. Phew! There were a few more hooded

CURZON TUNNEL

young men lurking around when I reached the other end, but they all seemed harmless. I thought it was all very odd until a friend told me Curzon Tunnel is where gay men meet for a bit of "fun". He seemed to know quite a lot on the subject, and what they were up to even has a name. "Cottaging". Well, that explains everything, and it's great to learn something new about the canals of Birmingham (and about my friend).

We're now on the Grand Union Canal, walking back towards Warwick and we pass the usual graffiti and familiar old industrial buildings, some brightened up with a lick of paint. Sorry, that's not going to stop them being knocked flat when the time comes. Ahead is where the canal splits and straight on would take us back to Warwick. But this time we go left, under the bridge, and head back to Garrison Lane.

FACTORY BUILDING SPANNING THE CANAL.

Soon, we come to a rundown factory building forming a tunnel and spanning the canal. Its rusty old corrugated panelling looks ready to drop, an ominous sign we're back in the "Hood" and on Peaky Blinders turf.

There's quite a lot of graffiti around here. A Banksy'esque piece of street art, with the tag "Tame'" and depicting a little girl holding a heart shaped balloon, appeared close by. Tame, real name Sam Opolli, died in 2013 when he fell from a building in Floodgate Street, very close to the canal. He was only 16. I wonder where the Banksy came from?

A solid, important looking Victorian red brick building called Phoenix Wharf majestically overlooks the towpath. I wonder what its original purpose was. We're back in Garrison Lane but can't leave without taking a quick look at the Garrison Tavern, Peaky Blinders' old watering hole. This Victorian boozer has certainly seen better days. It's closed down now, dilapidated and in need of a complete overhaul if it's to re-open. I heard it recently went to auction and fetched £20,000 above the sale guide price. Is that a bit of jiggery-pokery from Peaky Blinders gang boss Thomas Shelby?

GARRISON TAVERN, THE PEAKY BLINDERS LOCAL.

A raised female voice attracted my attention on the bus home. "… Dint yo ear wot I just said?" Then silence as she listened to her phone. "… are yo stoopid or sumink?" Silence as she listened some more. "… wot did I just say? .. They should NOT be arrestin' yo … yo wuz the one wot got attacked .. yo wuz just reportinit, init." A pause as she listened to her phone some more, and then she got really angry. "DON'T LETUM ARREST YO, DO YO EAR ME … I'll call yo lay-a luv. Bye." And with that, she hung up. Blimey, I thought that was bad enough, until she started telling the lady sitting next to her about her nephew. He was in prison and was murdered just before he should have been released. She started to explain about "taking it to Parliament", and I'm settling in for the next chapter when suddenly she says "see yo tomorra" and gets off at the next stop. I just sit there, gobsmacked. What must that lady and her family be going through? I wanted to follow her off the bus, hear the whole story and stay connected to find out what happens next. If you were able to swap your biggest problems with someone else's, would you? It certainly put my bucketful of problems into perspective, and I was glad to get home and count my blessings.

TEN

PEOPLE OF THE CANAL

I've encountered all sorts of interesting people whilst travelling the towpath. Somehow, the canal seems to attract independently minded individuals from all walks of life, and here, I'm going to attempt to give you a flavour of some of the people I've met. I'm not going to bother with the Gongoozler or canal walker or runner because I'm all of those things, and you must have got an idea of what I'm about by now. So, in no particular order, here goes.

The Narrowboater

I've spoken with plenty of narrowboaters whilst trudging the towpath, and on the whole, they're a great bunch of people. There's the occasional miserable, unfriendly git, but that's normal in any community. And it's definitely a community when you enter the narrowboating world. Narrowboaters fit into different categories. There are holidaymakers who simply rent a boat for a couple of weeks to experience the canals. Then you have boat owning holidaymakers, some sharing ownership, who use their boat for a few weeks a year, often travelling many miles, exploring Britain from a completely different angle. Or the boat owner who uses the boat as a weekend retreat, with the option to travel the canals whenever and wherever they fancy. A bit like a floating caravan, either static or touring. Some people like to live on a boat because the nomadic lifestyle suits them. But many more do so to reduce their outgoing expenses. I've heard the same story so many times, about not being able to get on the property ladder, so buying a boat is an alternative. But boat life still has its costs, and there are plenty more chores to consider. Like finding a hookup for the electricity supply, pumping in water, chopping wood for the fire and, best of all, offloading toilet waste. I got chatting to Gaz about canal life. We were both travelling the Oxford Canal, me on foot and him by narrowboat and he told me he was on his way to get his bottom scrubbed. He quickly explained it was for his boat when he saw my pained expression. I started asking him about life on the cut and he told me; *"... it's not everyone's cup of tea, especially in the winter when it's freezing ya cobblers off and ya need to empty the toilet and the dump station is miles away."* He also knows of people who just couldn't cope with living in such a confined space (there's a reason they're called narrowboats). And getting on with your partner is pretty important too if you're going to share the cramped living space. Here is a story from Rhiannon, new to living on the canal, who I met whilst walking the towpath into Birmingham one day. In her own words, she explains ...

"I'd never have guessed I'd be living on a boat, but options were limited for me and my partner. Our stash of cash simply wouldn't stretch to buying a house. After exploring a few ideas, we soon became proud but terrified owners of Bluebell, a 47ft narrowboat moored in Devises. With so many work commitments, we only had a tiny window of opportunity to bring our new floating home to Birmingham. Drama began when attempting an early morning departure and waking up the whole canalside community with our inability to steer, and our lack of control in reverse. After much instruction from our surprisingly jovial, sleep deprived neighbours, a lovely couple took us under their wing and showed us the ropes and we were finally on our way. From the Kennet and Avon Canal, we headed for Bath to join the River Avon where we would require the services of a pilot to navigate to Portishead. After an invigorating journey through the heart of Bristol, we moored up for the night. In the morning, at first tide, Mother Nature and our pilot did us proud, with tail winds and a pulling tidal grip helping Bluebell speed past cargo ships and sail the fastest

she ever will. Next day we arrived in Gloucester and discovered we must wait because the river is tidal. But the Lock Keeper and the Cosmos had other ideas. From that very morning, the river was NOT tidal and we were on our way. Anyone would have thought we'd planned it. Now on the home run, we arrived in Birmingham, exhausted but with days to spare. First impressions, Birmingham waterways are so much quieter, compared with the bustle of the Kennet & Avon canal. Canal culture is the same though. People are friendly and generous with their time, skills and advice, helping each other out when necessary. For us, it was invaluable. Life aboard is simpler but harder in varying measures. Sawing wood for the fire could seem an inconvenience, but it becomes part of a more real living existence. Our revolt against buying more "stuff", with modern society's continuous drive of consumerism, feels freeing. And not having any bills or post is a bonus too."

Many "live-a-boards" complain of lack of permanent moorings around the country. I've heard that if local residents complain, often the council will impose restrictions on moorings. I met Rosie and Steve along the Grand Union Canal. They were studying at Warwick University and the only mooring they could find was in Tipton, miles away. Not having a proper address caused problems, because they like the occasional Indian takeaway treat. To overcome this obstacle, they find a house close to a bridge on Google Maps. When they order the meal, they'll give the house address and ask it to be delivered "under the bridge". Where there's a will, there's a way. I was also chatting with Clare, an experienced live-aboard who explained what it's like for her living on a boat. *"Everything runs on 12 volt from the solar panel. Water-points can be sparse, so washing up is saved until there's enough for a full sink and the water has been engine-heated from travelling. Showering is economical ... soaping-up is always done with the water off. Changing the gas bottle can be a feat, climbing round the cratch* (translation = a kind of small cockpit). *In cooler months we need space for the coal and we keep the fire on tick-over. If it's gone out at the end of a working day, we just find a warm pub. Shopping involves two trolleys, stacked bags, straps and the nearest supermarket could be miles away. Space is limited and you realise you had too much stuff anyway. Oh, and then there are the spiders ... lots of spiders. But, the scenery you see, the people you meet, the exploring you can do and memories you make are fantastic."*

Talking to narrowboaters, there's a common thread; the kindness of others, always there to lend a fellow boater a hand. Oh, and another thing they have in common, the many mishaps, disasters and hilarious experiences I've heard have had me in stitches. Never a dull moment when you're narrowboating.

The Canal Trader

There are all sorts of traders operating from boats along the towpath. From fuel merchants to Christianity. Yes, Christianity. A narrowboat flying the "Boaters Christian Fellowship" flag is a regular around the Warwick Ring. The more ordinary offerings are; restaurant, café, water bus, boat trips, greetings cards, plants and flowers, gifts and crafts. Now this is unusual, a hotel in the canal? "Boatel" offer three rooms on their narrowboat moored in Gas Street Basin in the heart of Birmingham. Another interesting Birmingham canal trader is Cycle Chain, a social enterprise. They sell recycled bikes and offer a bike repair service too, all from "Carina", a converted, 72ft. cargo boat moored at Brindley Place. The crew is made up of part time volunteers, some of whom have experienced disability and personal challenges. Volunteers go through a thorough training programme and, together with practical experience on the boat, become competent bike mechanics. Julian, one of the Directors explained, *"We have had lots of success with students on the autistic spectrum, where our personal approach suits the student, who would usually find it difficult in a busy classroom setting."* They originally began with charity funding, but it's now a stand-alone enterprise. Most of the bikes they sell have been recovered by the Police and go through the repair shop to get them back into good working order. Any bikes beyond economical repair are donated for shipment to poor countries. So, it's hats off to the crew of "Carina" and volunteer Directors, Julian Cleaver and Mark Duce.

If there was a competition to see how many plants you could fit on top of a narrowboat, Claire and Neil would win. Walking past Jodarolo, their 57ft. narrowboat with its beautifully curved front end (Neil later told me it's a rare Hixon hull), I couldn't help but stop to take a closer look. The couple now live and trade on the canal, with Neil growing and nurturing the plants (all from seed), and Claire creating greetings cards and other works of art, which were on display in Jodarolo"s cabin windows. Their current annual route is from Nantwich to Banbury and they have their favorite stopping places where trade is good. Both are originally from Dorset, Neil with a background in sales, timber boat building and eventually, with his own workshop, specialising in windows, and Claire emigrated to Australia for a while, before returning to the UK and taking a post as Pensions Manager. They met, fell in love and decided to do something completely different with their lives. With no plan and very little time to think about it, they bought Jodarolo. That was seven years ago and now they are one of the happiest couples I have ever met, anywhere. I asked what their secret is and Claire said, " ... *our days don't have much of a structure ... we don't need much and we're very happy with our lot."* Neil added, *"Living on a canal boat as a couple, you need to be solid, no secrets, no hiding places ... and if you start bickering, it's time to move on."* Well, whatever it is they have, Neil should harvest it, Claire should bottle it and they both should sell it for lots of money.

The Cyclist

I'm not going to spend too much time talking about cyclists on the towpath because it's such a provocative subject, and I don't want to fall out with anyone. Most narrowboating non-cyclists I have spoken to get very agitated and opinionated when the subject comes up. Here is a very small sample of the kind of things they say.

Maggie said ... *"Our cat has had many near misses and we've almost been mowed over through the bridge holes."*

Steve said ... *"Cyclists should have a bell ... they usually don't work anyway."*

Robin said ... *"I've been hit twice. Bikers think they have the right of way. It's a towpath, not a bloody cyclepath."*

Tricia said ... *"It makes me very angry when they come up too fast and whizz past with no warning."*

Mike said ... *"I'll ride my bike wherever I want to. Get over it."*

Sylvia said ... *"Bikers? They're too fast, inconsiderate, rude and dangerous."*

Paul said … *"A biker dodged a dog and rode straight into my rope … ended up in the canal. It was so funny."*

Pete said … *"Yeah, some bikers can be annoying, so can some boaters, but the worst are those who don't clean up after their dogs."*

That's enough about cyclists and being as Pete mentioned dogs, our next subject is …..

The Dog Owner

You see a lot of dogs on the towpath. Consequently, there are lots of dog poo piles around. Some areas are particularly blighted, so, for a bit of entertainment on my lonely walks, I invented the "TURD ON THE TOWPATH AWARD" and made a mental note every time I encountered a particularly bad area. Either side of bridge 52 on the Coventry Canal in Polesworth was by far the worst I'd ever seen. A minefield of dog turds; absolutely disgusting. So, Polesworth instantly won my imaginary prize. I was walking along the canal near Polesworth recently and decided to talk to a dog owner about my imaginary award. My unfortunate victim was Craig, a responsible dog owner, who was carrying two bags of warm dog poo belonging to Daisy, his Staffordshire Bull Terrier. He said, *"It's not just the dog walkers, it's boaters too... it's a bloody nightmare but there's nothing much you can do about it."* I told him about the TURD ON THE TOWPATH AWARD (I didn't divulge it was made-up) and he just said *"Yup, Polesworth definitely deserves it."* This is a hot topic along the towpath and here is a sample of what other people have told me.

Debbie said … *"There's dog poo bins and signs up at the Marina saying £500 fine, but the culprits never get caught. Us dog owners have complained cuz we get a bad name."*

Linda said … *"What gets me are the ones who bag up the poo then hang it on a tree or leave it on the towpath."*

Lynda said … *"I clean up after my dog but frankly, lots of other animals do it too … what's the fuss?"*

Becky said … *"I cleared up about 15 piles on a neighbouring mooring. When the boat left, no more poo. But the same boat turns up next to me at another mooring and it starts again, right next to the ropes where I step off the boat."*

So, well done to the few inconsiderate cretins who give dog owners a bad name, sitting on their fat backsides, doing absolutely nothing as their darling pooches pile on the poo and seriously blight the towpath.

The Fisherman

After many, many miles of towpath travel, I've come to the conclusion that fishing is mainly a male sport. In fact, a middle aged, white male sport. I've seen one, maybe two Middle Eastern looking fishermen, but with very little in the way of fishing tackle. And I've only ever seen one fisher-lady. Now what I'm about to tell you is top secret. I promised Matt, a fisherman I got chatting to under Spaghetti Junction, when I asked him about fishing in such an urban setting. *"This stretch of canal is the best fishing in the area, probably the country. I've caught monster chub and carp."* I asked him about pike. *"Yes, there are plenty of pike around here. I hate them, most proper anglers do. I'm happy to see the Eastern Europeans catch 'em … they don't throw 'em back."* I asked him why that was and he said, *"because pike is like a Christmas delicacy for them."* Matt is worried about pollution affecting fish stock in some canal areas, and he is regularly offered cheap tv's, bikes and other random, knocked off contraband. When the weather is good, Matt will spend all day and most of the evening fishing. When it's time to go home, he'll finish his beer, pack up his tackle, weigh his catch and chuck 'em all back in the canal. That's the part I've never understood about fishing. After putting that much effort into catching the slimy little buggers, I'd take 'em home and have a stupendous feast. But that's illegal apparently. No, fishing isn't for me.

The Street Artist

When I stopped to admire the street art at bridge No.3 on the Coventry Canal, I got chatting to a chap by the name of Tim from Brink Contemporary Arts. He explained that Brink is a street art organization, responsible for transforming this once scruffy corner into a delightful oasis. Working in conjunction with the Canal and River Trust, they are transforming a few canalside areas around Coventry and beyond. Tim told me about his concern for some of the wonderful old canal brickwork which has been disfigured and spoilt by graffiti, and tagging in particular. I asked Tim if he had ever done any graffiti and he said he always asks for the owner's permission before starting any work. The artwork at bridge No.3 was pretty recent and had no added graffiti or tagging, but I wondered how Tim felt about people tagging or painting onto his artwork. He seemed pretty relaxed about it and said ... *"If they bring their 'A' game and its really good work, that's okay, but inferior, scruffy or juvenile work, or tagging for tagging sake, then it's not really that cool."* Tim graduated from Birmingham School of Art with a Masters Degree and is now a practicing artist and street art curator. Interestingly, where good street art has been added to run down city areas in other parts of the country, it has helped to reduce litter, graffiti and anti-social behaviour. And in some areas, public art has actually increased the value of private property. Anyway, the locals I spoke to who passed by all loved it.

The Graffiti Artist.

Is graffiti art or vandalism? 2,500 year old erotic graffiti was found on a Greek island in 2014. Was that art or vandalism? Most people I speak to hate graffiti. Walking into Birmingham, along the towpath, you are bombarded by graffiti leaping out from ugly factory walls and fences. Some of it is exceptional and some is rubbish, but most of it is doing no harm at all. It's a place where talented youngsters come to exercise and develop their creative muscles and I want to find out more. It's an illegal activity, so how do I find a Graffiti Artist for a chat? I had almost given up on the idea when I happened to be passing some street art and got chatting to a fella who turned out to be in the graffiti "business". He explained that a proper graffiti artist is called a Graffiti Writer. Someone who just scrawls a tag (their identifying name) is a Tagger. The silver and black graffiti is done very quickly by a Dubber, and whoever produces really poor work is called a Toy. The best, most respected Graffiti Writers are called Kings and will include a crown in their work. Chris, who's tag is MEFOE, started painting on walls in the 80's and was attracted to it by the Hip Hop culture coming out of New York. He told me that often, the police would turn a blind eye to graffiti in run down areas. But the policy would often change, and police would suddenly come down hard on anyone they caught. Chris has friends who went to prison for their crime. He also knows of sought-after graffiti writers, travelling the world and making a lot of money from their art. The thrill for the graffiti writer is for as many people as possible to see their work, whilst they remain anonymous. Finding a "blank canvas" which is very visible, but difficult to reach is the ultimate. Council workers can't destroy it and other graffiti writers can't paint over it. In pursuit of that perfect location can be very dangerous and lives have been lost. To avoid detection, most of Chris's work was done in the early hours of the morning, but security cameras make things a lot more risky. Chris is in his 40's and works for himself, so taking risks is not an option. He now practises his art in areas untroubled by the authorities. He tells me the graffiti community has its rules. No graffiti on churches, graveyards, clean property or clean houses. Respect "Kings" and learn from them and do not tag someone else's work. Violence can erupt when someone tags someone else's work, and in the old days, it could end with a few harsh words or the occasional punch up. But now, with knives so common amongst the young, there have been stabbings in retaliation. Well, after my brief graffiti education, I will walk along the towpath into Birmingham with a fresh pair of eyes and loads more knowledge. Thanks MEFOE.

The Magnet Fishermen

Hello, what are these two blokes doing along the Oxford Canal near Rugby? Oh, they're magnet fishing. There are piles of odd bits of metal debris at various bridges along the towpath, and it's all because of the new "sport" of magnet fishing. Tie a big magnet to a piece of rope, chuck it into a canal and, hey presto, you're a Magnet Fisherman. Before he had chance to chuck his magnet back into the water, I asked one of the guys, Dave, what it's all about. He'd recently taken up the "sport" and was trying to emulate local man, Paul Price, who has recovered rifles, revolvers, submachine guns, swords, a Vespa scooter, a couple of safes and a hand grenade. The Bomb Squad were called in to deal with the grenade. To date, Dave told me he has pulled out a very nice, almost vintage baked bean tin in excellent condition. I asked the other bloke how he's getting on and he just stared back at me with a vacant expression. It takes all sorts.

The Homeless

When walking the towpath on one of the coldest mornings of the year, I noticed a rough sleeper tidying up around his tent. He looked frozen, so I went over to check he was okay and ended up staying for a chat. He was very open about his situation and told me he lives on the street to avoid the druggies who reside at the homeless shelters. Yes, he's done drugs and drink ... been to prison ... goes to church ... shits in a plastic bag to keep the place clean ... one of 7 kids ... Dad left when he was 5 ... he has 4 kids ... loves his mum ... has had money, tent and sleeping bag stolen ... he's a soft touch for a hard luck story ... etc., etc. His name is Jason, and he's been living at this spot for around 4 months, but thinks he'll be moved on soon. Whilst I was there, a car stopped (we were close to a main road) and a lady handed him a mug of coffee, sandwiches and a hot water bottle. Later, a couple of Police Officers paid him a visit and I was expecting trouble. But they only wanted to know if he'd seen an incident, which had happened the night before. After sharing my lunch with Jason, I left, promising to bring him coffee and sandwiches next time, but not a hot water bottle. Good luck Jason.

ELEVEN

LAPWORTH TO BIRMINGHAM

18 MILES

Bill Savage

Today, we're going to walk a different route into Birmingham, starting at Kingsbury Junction in Lapworth where we join the Stratford Canal. Businessmen in Stratford-upon-Avon feared the canal network was passing them by and so built this canal. It was authorised in 1793 but completion was not until 1816, and within another 20 years, the railway was taking trade away. The Great Western Railway eventually bought the canal, mainly for the water supply, and their triangular signs can still be seen along the towpath. Unique to the Stratford Canal are the round roofs of lock-keepers cottages. The craftsmen who built them were so used to building barrel-vaulted bridges, the same technique was used for the cottage roofs. There are some unusual sights along this route including three drawbridges, an unusual number of split bridges and a guillotine lock. The split bridge was cheap to build and designed to allow the rope to pass through the middle of the bridge to avoid unhitching the horse from the boat.

SPLIT BRIDGE & LOCK KEEPERS COTTAGE.

It's a late start due to Storm Eleanor shaking us up last night, with her 100 miles per hour winds, but this morning is a little calmer. The canal was covered in ice the last time I was here, and in the past, people would skate on it if thick enough. But, after church on Ash Wednesday in 1907, a bunch of kids decided to go sliding on the nearby pond. The weather had been getting warmer and the ice thinner and, suddenly, the ice broke and four children drowned. The winter of 1962/63 was particularly cold and the canals iced over, stopping traffic and causing havoc. Some say this was the excuse they were looking for to close the canals for good.

Robert Catesby, the leader of the Gunpowder Plotters was born in Lapworth. We're just passing the Lapworth Cricket Club and I'm sure Robert would have captained the team if the game was around in his time. Next is an unusual working drawbridge and then another of a different design, both to allow farm access to and from the Old Warwick Road. Up ahead, floating in the middle of the canal is a large branch, brought down by the high winds. A man with a long skinny branch is attempting to catch it. He tells me he only came out for a newspaper but saw the branch and is now very worried it may do some damage to a passing boat, so he's working hard to get it to the bank. I offer to lend a hand and we are eventually successful. Getting it out of the water proves difficult though and I end up putting my foot into a puddle deeper than my boot. As we drag it out and I lift my end into the air to place it off the towpath and onto higher ground, dirty cold canal water dribbles down both arms. Ahhhh. I see my new friend isn't doing much lifting. After tidying up, we part company and I notice I'm covered in mud with soggy cold sleeves and water sloshing around in my left boot. On the other hand, he is completely unmarked in his brand new (it looks like a Christmas present) sheepskin gilet and light tan slacks. Even his boots look newly polished. How do I get myself into these pickles? Oh well. At least I've done my bit to save a boat from sinking.

Just over the next field are Earlswood Lakes, three reservoirs built in 1820 to feed and regulate canal water levels. It's been raining heavily for the last few days and you can see why these reservoirs are so important, in drought conditions, too. We've now come to Shirley Drawbridge at Majors Green, it's believed to be the only working road drawbridge left in England. When a canal boat wants to go through, the boatman activates traffic lights, which stop the traffic. Narrowboats are slow creatures and road users must get pretty frustrated in the summer, when it's busy.

SHIRLEY DRAW BRIDGE

The aqueduct, which regularly floods the road below during the winter is next, but it's okay today. There are plenty of residential properties along this route. Many are new and some developers have incorporated the canal as a trendy, waterfront feature. The older properties are built the other way around, with their backs facing the canal and gardens going down to the water's edge. Some even have their own moorings and boats.

Whilst it's quiet, I think it's time to "big up" the Canal Navvy. Engineers may have designed the canals, but it was left to vast gangs of navvies to build them. At one stage in the 19th century, one in every 100 working people in the UK was a navvy and they were the highest paid manual workers in the land. Navvies worked hard and drank hard. "Going on a randy" was navvy slang for going on a drinking spree that could last several days. They survived by drinking gallons of weak beer and eating bread and potatoes. The men got accommodation when and where they could, and it was only rarely in a proper building or bed. They worked long hours, in difficult conditions with nothing but their own strong arms and the simplest of tools - just pickaxe and shovel. Getting the job done was far more important than safety and many navvies were killed. The widow of a dead navvy might get £5 compensation if she was lucky, and that's only if the employer had a proper record of the individual. After the canal, work continued with the building of the railway. When that dried up, they sought work across the Channel where British navvies frequently got paid twice as much as anybody else, simply because they worked twice as hard. The canal system we enjoy today was created just as much by the ingenious engineers as by the hard work and deprivation of the navvy. And let's not forget the stonemason, carpenter and blacksmith, who also did pretty well out of the creation of the canals.

What on earth is this? A smartly dressed lady is walking her trouser wearing dog along the towpath, so I stop to admire the spectacle. She tells me "Poppy", for that is the dog's name, used to get very muddy during a walk. She is a Rough Collie (dog, not owner), very hairy (dog, not owner) and a nightmare to clean (dog, not owner). Wow, they both looked very posh and slightly out of place around here. I wonder if dog trousers will catch on?

POPPY IN TROUSERS

There's a big hill directly ahead and it looks like a dead end. This must be Brandwood Tunnel, and it's a long one. 322 metres with no towpath. The poor toerags would be in the tunnel for quite a while before getting to the other side. The longest tunnel, the Standedge on the Huddersfield Canal, was built in 1794 and is 5210 metres long. Wow, that's over three miles in old money. Three cheers for King Navvy. Once you walk the long path to street level, it's a jungle up there. All you see are houses, traffic lights, a busy junction and a row of shops. I know from experience, only luck and local knowledge will get you through to the other side. After scratching my head for a while the first time I was here, I went looking for a local guide. I asked a couple of people at the bus stop and then at the local shops, but no one was able to help. So, I went searching for "the other side" and ended up in someone's back garden. Realising I could easily be mistaken for a burglar (I do look like a scruffy tramp with swag bag on my back on these walks), I decided to give up and head back home. Whilst waiting at the bus stop, a group of exuberant schoolkids appeared and I thought, if anyone knows, they will. Eventually, after a bit of argy-bargy and an excited discussion (the kids, not me), I got directions. I was miles away and at first thought the kids were having a bit of fun with me (they're not like my Rugby School chums you know), but after carefully following their directions, I found the path out of the jungle and eventually reached familiar ground, the towpath. Actually, like most kids, these kids were great and enjoyed the opportunity to help a lost soul.

We've almost reached Kings Norton where we join the Worcester and Birmingham Canal and here, we encounter our first derelict factory of the day. I spot a graffiti'd up factory door, some gorgeous flaky paint work on an old cast iron pipe running along the top of some rusty old window frames, complete with broken glass. Time to get the camera out. Before taking any shots, I let a group of grey haired, lady walkers go by. As they pass, they look at the camera, then turn to see what I'm photographing, turn back and give me a quizzical look. So, I say "beauty is in the eye of the beholder". They look pityingly back at me and scurry on, with the occasional backwards glance.

A little further along the towpath, just before the junction of the two canals, is a rare guillotine lock, constructed in 1814, around the time when Napoleon was rattling his cage. There are a few on East Anglia waterways but this is the only guillotine stop lock on the canal network and was built to regulate a height difference of 1 inch between the two canals.

GUILLOTINE LOCK

The plan is to turn right at the junction and carry on into Birmingham. But first, let's have a quick look at Wast Hills Tunnel, just a short distance up the Worcester Canal. I heard recently that a narrowboat travelling out of the tunnel was pelted from above with bricks and bottles. Charming. Also, a

WAST HILLS TUNNEL

canoeist is known to have died in his attempt to get through. Blimey! And it looks so peaceful and innocent. At 2726 yards long (that's over a mile and a half), it's one of the longest on the UK canal network. It was built in 1796, with no adjacent towpath, so must have been pretty tiring for the poor fellas legging it through. One hell of a trip for the horses too, over the hills to the other end of the tunnel. Interestingly, Birmingham City Football Club training ground sits atop.

In the 19th century, Kings Norton was a rural area with a cattle market and mills on the River Rea for grinding corn. With the arrival of the canals and then the railway, the area quickly changed to take advantage of this new transport hub. A paper mill and then chemical works were the first factory buildings along here.

Bournville Railway Station, decked out in Cadbury colours, sits right next to the canal and we'll be passing the massive Cadbury factory soon. John Cadbury produced his first drinking chocolate in 1824 for his shop in Birmingham. One of his early factories was in Bridge Street, close to Gas Street Basin, where it had its own spur to the canal. When John became ill and retired in 1861, the business employed only 11 people and was losing money. His two sons took over and wanted to move production out of the smoke of industrial Birmingham. Cadbury was reliant on the canals for milk and the railway for cocoa and Bournville proved to be a perfect location, with both on the doorstep. The factory opened in 1879 and Cadbury became famous not just for its chocolate, but also for the advances in conditions and social benefits for its workforce. In 2010, after a hostile bid, USA food giant Kraft bought the company. Shareholders were generally delighted with their windfall, but the Cadbury family and company management didn't want to sell. The unions were also worried. Kraft made promises not to close a particular factory but, soon after taking over, the factory closed. Other "manipulations" include rounding chocolate bar corners and other tricks to reduce weight, but not appearance, fiddling with recipes, moving some production to Poland, but still printing the Union Jack on the wrappers and - the meanest trick of all - scrapping the Cadbury pensioners' long-standing chocolate Christmas treat. So much for the Cadbury family's ethical ideals. Cadburys World and some other facilities remain in Bournville, for now.

Building of the Worcester and Birmingham Canal was completed in 1815. From 1841, competition from the railways decimated the canal trade and in 1868 losses were so severe that a receiver was appointed. In 1874 the canal was sold to the Sharpness New Docks Company. The last commercial cargo in the early 1960s was coal from Cannock to Worcester and chocolate crumb from Worcester to Bournville. During the late 1960's, prison labourers were used to get the canal back into good condition for recreational use. From here, the rail track runs parallel with the canal for much of the route into Birmingham. Most of the supplies for building the railway were shipped by canal and it must have been soul-destroying for the canal people to watch the railway being built only a few feet away, destroying their livelihood and way of life.

CANAL AND RAIL SIDE
BY SIDE

We're now passing through Selly Oak, where the Dudley No.2 Canal once connected with the Worcester and Birmingham Canal. I once attempted to walk it (around 7.5 miles) but only got about half way. The canal slowly petered out and disappeared behind houses somewhere in Halesowen. Sadly, there is no sign of the junction today, but I've heard talk of restoration starting at the Selly Oak end. I live in hope.

In 1872, a large workhouse for the poor was built here, to replace those in five surrounding parishes. The thinking at the time was that if conditions in the workhouse were really bad, it would deter the poor from seeking relief and force them to get a job. Eventually, it became clear that the majority of workhouse inmates were the young, the old, the chronically sick and the mentally ill. In effect, the most vulnerable people in society. Acts of Parliament led to separate provisions for children and the mentally ill. An infirmary built next to the workhouse was provided for poor people who were sick, and many parish or local hospitals originate from this arrangement.

I was walking the towpath the other day when a bloke started stalking me. When I stopped, he stopped. A little later, I noticed him again. It was early, and the towpath was empty, apart from me and my stalker. I was taking a couple of photos and eventually forgot all about him. Until, that is, he scurried past, gave me a sideways scowl and said ... *"You was worryin' me there mate ... stoppin' an' a-startin' like that ... there's some dodgy geezers 'round 'ere ... can't be too careful ... bloody late for work now"*. With that, he quickened his pace and was gone.

It's me looking like a "dodgy geezer" is it? Pot calling kettle black I'd say.

This route into Birmingham is far more genteel compared with the Grand Union route and the view makes a change from derelict factories, graffiti fences and barbed wire. The canal flows through an aqueduct along here so we're high up and have excellent views of both sides. We're passing through Edgbaston, which is only a couple of miles out of the city and is home to Queen Elizabeth Hospital, The University of Birmingham and Edgbaston Cricket Ground (home to Warwickshire County Cricket Club). The old hospital, named after Queen Elizabeth the Queen Mother, was opened in the late 1930's and marked a new departure for medicine in Birmingham, linking hospital and academic medicine on a single site. It was replaced in 2010 with a new facility and is one of the largest single site hospitals in Britain with the largest solid organ transplant programme in Europe, the largest renal transplant programme in Britain and the largest single floor critical care unit in the world. Looking down from the vantage point of the towpath, it all looks mighty impressive.

Just before Edgbaston Tunnel is a mooring area for The University of Birmingham where you can catch a boat into the city. That's handy. After the tunnel, familiar sights start to appear on the horizon. Although it's getting dark, the BT Tower is clearly visible. It's great to see the bright lights of the city reflecting in the canal water. Gas Street Basin and a sit down can't be far now.

The towpath is a great place to keep fit. Some GP's are 'prescribing' a walk along the canal to help lower blood pressure, fight depression and combat chronic lung conditions. And the charity 'Mind' has organised canal walks to improve mental health. Just remember to give passing boaters, walkers, runners, cyclists, anglers and gongoozlers a cheery wave.

KEEPING FIT ALONG
BIRMINGHAM'S
CANALS.

The first coal to arrive in Birmingham from the Black Country was on 6th November 1769, helping the city to become the "Workshop of the World" and "The City of a Thousand Trades".

From small, one-man bands to industrial giants, Birmingham goods were shipped across the globe. And it would have been impossible without the canal to bring in coal, iron and other heavy goods to feed this humongous manufacturing monster. Within the City of Birmingham alone there are 56 kilometres of canal, which, at its peak in 1898, carried eight and a half million tons of cargo. Like Coventry, Birmingham was heavily reliant on the motor industry, which was initially brought to its knees during the 1970's recession and has continued its decline ever since. Despite the knocks, Birmingham has not lost its mojo and was recently identified as the top city in the U.K. for the greatest number of new inventions. It's also the youngest city in Europe, with under-25s accounting for nearly 40% of the population.

We are so lucky to have such a rich vein of history to dip into as we walk the Warwick Ring. How many world firsts, world's biggest and world-changing stuff have we uncovered on this short trip around the Warwick Ring? And we've hardly scratched the surface. From the first iron steamboat to the first man-made fibres, the biggest motorbike manufacturer to the biggest critical care unit, and with William Webb Ellis and Frank Whittle both changing the world with the game of rugby and the turbojet engine, it's all happening around this 115 mile route of the Warwick Ring. The rise and fall of our industries is plain for all to see, but brought into sharp focus when walking through the once wealth-creating districts of two manufacturing giants, Coventry and Birmingham. It's also interesting to discover how many useful substances were plucked from the ground all around the Warwick Ring. Granite and quartzite for road building, sand and gravel, limestone for cement-making, clay for bricks and of course, colossal amounts of coal. Essential ammunition for the Industrial Revolution, in plentiful supply and within easy reach.

This is it, Gas Street Basin, the end of our journey and where we part company. I expect to be walking these towpaths for a little while yet, witnessing the inevitable changes to the landscape and discovering even more about the local history embedded around this canal route. Every time I walk along the canal, I am awestruck by the sheer magnitude of the task of constructing this 18th-century superhighway. Two hundred and fifty years ago there were no satellites or software to work out the best route, or earth-moving equipment to construct a path. Concrete wasn't developed until 1849 and the only means of transport across the land was by horse or on foot. What about those neat tunnels too? All done by hand (and a little gunpowder I expect). Whatever the obstacle; hill, valley or river, the unstoppable navvy just carried on. Now, 250 years later, town and city planners must succumb to the canal, making way for its flow unimpeded. CANAL IS KING.

GAS STREET BASIN WITH BRINDLEY PLACE THROUGH THE TUNNEL.

Canal is King

Printed in Poland
by Amazon Fulfillment
Poland Sp. z o.o., Wrocław

62657569R00114